CW01024716

Greek Folk Tales

Greek Folk Tales

Translated by
Alexander Zaphiriou

Illustrated by
Panagiotis Stavropoulos

AIORA

Alexander Zaphiriou studied Comparative Literature at Columbia University, in New York. He has worked as an interpreter for the Council of Europe, the IMF, and other international organizations since the '90s. He has translated fiction and non-fiction from and to English and Greek. His compilation *Myths Behind Words* was published by Aiora Press in 2018.

ISBN: 978-618-5369-74-3

First edition June 2023
Reprinted January 2024

AIORA PRESS
11 Mavromichali St.
Athens 10679 - Greece
tel: +30 210 3839000
www.aiorabooks.com

Table of Contents

The folk tales included in this volume were collected in the late-nineteenth to mid-twentieth century. They were found in Greek-speaking lands, including Asia Minor and Cyprus. A few have been borrowed from traditions beyond Greece, while some have come down to us from antiquity, including Aesop-like fables with speaking animal characters.

New Tunes

Alexander the king, having fought his wars and conquered all the dominions in the world, and finding the whole inhabited earth atremble in fear of him, called his soothsayers and asked, 'Tell me, you who know the writings of destiny, what should I do to live many a long year and have my pleasure in the world, now that I've made it all my own?'

'O my king, may your life be long, your power is formidable,' replied his soothsayers, 'but what is ordained by destiny cannot be undone. There's one thing only that can be done to make you have pleasure in your domains and in your renown and glory too, so that you may seek to be immortal and live as long as mountains do. But it is hard, exceedingly hard.'

'I'm not asking you whether it's hard, just what it is,' said Alexander.

'Well then, O king, as you please. It is the undying water, and who drinks of it fears not death. But any who seek to obtain it must pass between two mountains that clash on one another without ceasing. Not even a bird can slip through. Numberless renowned princes and nobles have lost their life in that awful snare! Once you've passed through the two mountains there's an unsleeping dragon guarding the undying water. Just slay the dragon and it's yours.'

Straightaway Alexander ordered that his steed Bucephalus be brought to him. The horse, though wingless, flew like a bird. He mounted, set his spurs and off they went. And with a swish of his crop they passed through the two mountains. He slew the unsleeping dragon and grabbed the glass that held the undying water.

But what was the use? For when he got back to his palace he didn't look after it properly! His sister saw it and, with nary a thought about what it might be, she poured it out. And it so happened that it landed on a wild onion, which is why wild onions never perish.

Some while later Alexander went to drink the undying water, but where had it gone? He asked his sister and she told him she'd no idea what it was and had poured it away. The king nearly went mad with wrath and distress, and cursed her to become a fish from the waist down and to be stranded in the middle of the sea, tormented for as long as the world should be.

God heeded this, and since that time those who sail in ships see her tossed amidst the waves. Still, she has no hate for Alexander and when she sees a ship she asks, 'Is Alexander still alive?' And if the skipper is untutored and replies, 'He's dead,' the lass, such is her grief, makes a huge commotion in the sea with her flailing arms and her loose long blonde hair that the ship goes down. But those in the know will tell her, 'He's alive and he reigns over the world,' and then the poor lass is of good cheer and happily sings sweet songs.

That's where sailors pick up their new tunes and bring them to us.

The Twelve Months

Once upon a time a widow, who was awfully poor, had five children. So poor was she that there was nothing for her to hope for under the sun. And she couldn't find a job, save once a week a grand lady, who was her neighbour, had her in to knead the dough for her bread. For her pains she gave her nothing—no, not even the end crust of a loaf to bring to her children for them to eat. And the poor soul would leave with bits of dough sticking to her hands, and she would arrive home and wash them in clear water, and then she'd boil the water, which had become a kind of thin gruel, and her children had it as their meal. And with this gruel they ate their fill all week long, until their mother would knead the dough the following week and return home with her hands ready to wash so she could obtain the gruel once again.

And the grand lady's children, despite all the diverse fine dishes they were served and the wholesome bread that they ate, got no nourishment and were as thin as sprats. But the children of the poor widow got their sustenance and grew sturdy like little mullets. And the grand lady didn't know what to make of it all and talked about the matter with her friends, and here is what they said to her:

'The poor woman's children are nourished and thrive because she carries away the good fortune of your children on her hands and takes it to her own children. That's why hers grow rapidly while yours fall behind and can't make well.'

The grand lady gave credence to this and, when the day came round again to knead the dough, she didn't let the poor woman leave with her hands unwashed, but had her clean them thoroughly so that the good fortune wouldn't leave the house. The poor woman arrived home with her eyes brimming with tears.

The children saw her in a state, and also saw that her hands had no bits of dough sticking to them and began blubbering. There they were all wailing, and there was she, their mother, in tears. Until she, as a grown-up, stilled her heart and calmed herself and said to her children, 'Now, now, you calm down my children and quit your blubbing and I'll fetch you a hunk of bread.'

And she betook herself from door to door, and it was ages ere she found somebody to give her the end crust of a loaf. She took it home and dunked it in water and shared it among her children, and after they had eaten she put them to bed and they fell asleep. At midnight she made herself scarce, lest she had to look upon her children starving to death.

Now, as she was going through the wilderness in the middle of the night, she saw a rise and a glow atop of it. And as she drew close she saw that it was a tent, and in its middle there was a big chandelier with twelve branches, and under it was hanging something round, like a ball. She went into the tent and saw sitting there twelve lads talking about the affairs of one of them and what they ought to be doing about them.

The tent was round and, to the right of the entrance, there were three lads sitting with shirts unbuttoned, their arms full of tender grass shoots and branches in bloom.

Beyond them were another three, their sleeves rolled up to their elbows, wearing no jackets, and their arms filled with sheaves of ripe wheat.

Further down were another three lads, each one holding a bunch of grapes.

And beyond them were another three lads, scrunched up and wearing long fur coats from right up at their necks to below their knees.

When the lads beheld the woman they said, 'Welcome, Auntie, come and join us, and sit you down.'

And, after greeting them, the woman sat down. And once she had taken a seat they asked her how it came about that she found herself in those parts. And the poor widow told them about her situation and her suffering and, as the lads realized that she was famished, one of the ones in fur got up and laid her a table, and she ate; and she noticed that he had a limp.

After she had eaten and her hunger was sated the lads got to asking her all manner of things about the land and the woman responded as well as she could.

Eventually the three lads that were bare-chested asked, 'Hey, Auntie, how do you fare during the months of the year? What do you think of March and April and May?'

'We have a right good time, my children,' responded the widow, 'and in fact, when those months come, the hills and the meadows go green, and the earth is graced with all kinds of flowers and there's a fragrance everywhere that's enough to raise the dead. All the birds start chirping and twittering. The tillers of the soil see their fields go green and their hearts rejoice and they get their barns ready. So there's nothing to complain about as to March, April and May, lest God send a bolt from heaven and blast us for our ingratitude.'

So then the three lads in their shirtsleeves, who were holding their sheaves of wheat, took up the questions: 'Well, and what about Reaper and Thresher and August? What about them?'

And the poor woman responded, 'During those months there's nothing worth complaining about, because with the hot weather, the fruits of the earth ripen and all the bounty of the orchards ripens. That is when the farmers reap their crops and the garden produce is gathered. And the poor folk are well pleased with those months for they have no need then of many or costly things to wear.'

And then the three lads who were holding the grapes asked her in their turn, 'And what have you to say of September, October and November?'

'Those are the months,' said the woman, 'when people gather grapes and press them and make wine. And also, the good thing about them is that they signal the coming of winter and people see to it that they gather wood and charcoal and heavy clothing so as to keep warm.'

And the lads in furs asked her, 'So what about December, January and February? How are things then?'

'Ah, those months love us well,' said the poor woman, 'and we also love them a great deal. You may well ask, why? Well, here is why! Because people are insatiable of their nature and want to work the year round to earn a lot. Those winter months come round and gather us in around the hearth and give us respite from summer's toil. People love them also because, with their rains and snowfalls, they make the crops grow all over the fields. So, my children, all the months are good and worthy, and each one does its job as ordained by God. It's us humans that aren't sufficiently good.'

Then eleven of the lads made a sign to the first of the ones holding the grapes, and he went out and presently came back in, and in his hands he was holding a stoppered jar, and he gave it to the woman.

The lads said to her, 'So now, Auntie, get you on your way, and go home to care for your children, and take this jar along with you.'

The woman heaved the jar on her shoulder gladly, and said to the lads, 'May your years be full and right long, my children.'

'Good morrow to you, Auntie,' they said, and she was on her way.

And at exactly the hour that dawn was breaking, she arrived back home and found her children still asleep. She spread out a bedsheet and emptied the jar and found it to be filled with florins and she almost lost her wits for joy.

Once it was light, she went to the bakery in the market and bought half a dozen loaves of bread and a couple of pounds of cheese and wakened her children, washed them, got them dressed properly, had them say their prayers and then gave them bread and cheese, and the poor mites ate and had their proper fill.

Then she bought two pounds of wheat and took it to the mill and had it milled, and kneaded it and took the loaves to the baker to have them baked.

And as she was returning from the baker's with her tray of loaves on her shoulder, the grand lady chanced upon her and surmised that some windfall had happened, by good fortune, and went after her to find out how she'd got hold of the flour and had the bread baked. The poor, guileless woman told her the whole truth.

The grand lady felt envious and resolved to visit those lads herself.

So that very night, once she got her husband and children off to sleep, she stepped out of her mansion and took the road and went on until she found the tent where the twelve months dwelt and she greeted them.

And they said to her, 'Welcome, your ladyship. Why have you deigned to visit us?'

'La, sirs, it's because I'm deprived,' she replied, 'and have come to seek your help.'

'Very well,' they said. 'Are you hungry? Would you like something to eat?'

'No, no, thank you,' she said. 'I'm quite full up.'

'Very well,' said the lads, 'and might we ask how you manage things in town?'

'Couldn't be worse,' she replied.

'And how are you coping with the months?' they asked again.

'How do you expect us to cope?' said she. 'Each one has its own kind of ire. Once we've got used to the heat of August, here comes September all in haste, trailing October and November at its feet, and they chill us to the bone, and there you have this fellow in ague and that one getting the sniffles. Then, before you know it, it's winter, and December and January and February freeze us, and the lanes fill with snow, so we can't go out and about, especially in that lame old February!' (Poor February heard this and was quite mortified).

'And what of those flibbertigibbets, March, April and May! They don't realize they are summer months; they feign they be winter, and so winter ends up being nine months long. And we can't go out on May Day to have our coffee with milk and roll around in the grass.

Then there's the Reaper and the Thresher and August. They again have this thing of stifling us, till we are dripping with sweat with all the heat they bring. And indeed from the scorching heat of the Feast of the Assumption, there's this upheaval with the days of ill-omen that spoil our washing laid out to dry upon the flats. What can I tell you lads? Under the months we lead a blighted life.'

The lads said nothing but each made a sign to the one sitting in the middle of those that held the sheaves of wheat. He got up and fetched a stoppered jar, handed it to the woman and said, 'Take this jar and when you get home lock yourself alone inside a room and empty it. Don't you go opening it while you're still on the road.'

'Oh no, I wouldn't do that,' she said and left and arrived home before dawn, bursting with joy.

She locked herself in a room, spread out a bedsheet, took the lid off the jar and emptied it. And what came out of it? Masses of seething serpents! They all rushed to her and ate her alive. And she left her children orphaned, for it is not good for anyone to speak ill of another. But the poor woman, with her kind heart and honeyed tongue, became really well-to-do, a true gentlewoman, and did well for herself and for her children. There! This is what people call a good ending.

Myrsina

Once upon a time there were three sisters and, as it happened, they were orphans. They had neither mother nor father.

One day they wished to find out who was the fairest among the three of them. And as the sun was close to setting they got themselves to a spot where he shone on them. They stood in a line, the three of them, and said to the sun, 'O sun, O glorious sun, of us three who is the fairest?' And the sun said, 'This one's good and t'other one's good but the third one, the littlest one, she's the best of all.'

On hearing this the elder sisters felt a pang of jealousy, and they returned home in a foul mood.

The following day those two put on their Sunday best and, as for the youngest one, whose name was Myrsina, they got her up in the shabbiest clothes, dirty and worn, and went again to ask the sun.

And when they found themselves at their sun-drenched spot, they said again: 'O sun, O glorious sun, of the three of us who is the fairest?'

And the sun, again, said, 'This one's good and t'other one's good but the third one, the littlest one, she's the best of all.'

When Myrsina's sisters heard this they were as if singed, and returned home in a bitter mood.

And again, on the third day they queried the sun and he said the same thing once more. And they were fired up and inflamed, the two of them, with jealousy, and resolved to do away with poor little Myrsina.

'It's been ever so many years since our mother died, and we'll be getting up early at dawn to go quickly and bury her again,[1] but we need to get everything ready from the eve, for Mother is buried far, far away, atop the mountain, and we must set out without delay.'

Poor Myrsina believed it all and at the following daybreak they took with them a shewbread as offering and a bowl of wheatmeal for the dead and they set off to go and bury their mother again.

On and on they walked, and they walked and they reached the inside of a wood and arrived under a beech tree.

Then the eldest one said, 'Behold, here is our mother's grave. Fetch me the mattock to dig with.'

'Oh!' said the other one. 'Look now, and see what we've gone and done, such galoots that we are! What do

[1] The reburial of human skeletal remains has been common in Greece since at least the Mycenaean period.

we dig with? Neither a pitchfork nor a shovel did we bring! What do we do now?'

Then the eldest one said, 'One of us will have to go back and fetch the mattock!'

'I'm too scared,' said the middle one.

'And as for me,' said Myrsina, 'just a flying bird were I to see, all of a sudden, and I'd freeze up.'

'Listen here,' said the eldest one. 'You, Myrsina, shall stay here, and we'll fetch the mattock, for none of us dare go alone. Now, you stay here and keep watch over the boiled wheatmeal offering until we return.'

'Alright, but mind you return soon, for I'm scared of being alone.'

'No sooner said than done. We'll be off and then we'll be right back!' they said and left merrily.

Poor little Myrsina resigned herself to waiting, and she waited, and she waited until the sun went down. Then, when she realized that night was falling and that she was left all alone there on the mountain, she started crying. So much did she cry and wail that the trees themselves took pity on her.

One beech tree said to her, 'Don't you cry, my dear. Just roll that ring-loaf of yours and where it comes to a standstill that's where you can stay, and you be afraid of naught.'

So Myrsina rolled the loaf and ran after it. Would it stop here? Would it stop there? Without quite realizing it Myrsina found herself at the bottom of a dip. And lo, before her there was a house, so she went inside.

In that house lived twelve brothers, the months, and throughout each day they roamed the wide world and returned home each evening very, very late. And now that Myrsina had come there was no one there.

So then, without a moment's delay, Myrsina rolled up her sleeves, took up the broom, swept the entire house and then began cooking a lovely meal. Then she set the table, had something to eat and hid herself in the loft.

At that very moment the months turned up. They came inside and… what a surprise! The house spick and span; the table laid in readiness! Well, how about that!

And they said, 'Who is it that has done us this bit of kindness? Let them be afraid of nothing. If they come forth and are a boy, we'll make him our brother, and if it's a girl we'll have her for our sister.'

But there was no reply. So they had their meal and wondered all the while, and then they went to sleep.

In the morning they got up, full of beans, and went out, all of them. Then Myrsina came down from her hiding place, swept the entire house clean and set herself to bake a pie. And what a pie it was! A pie so delicious you had to lick your fingers clean. Then, as night fell, she laid the table and spread out everything beautifully. She cut herself a tiny piece of pie, ate and went again to hide in the loft.

A short while later the months got back, and when they saw everything in readiness they hardly knew how to react.

And this is what they said: 'But who is it then that's doing us this kindness? Let them show themselves; they need not fear; they've nothing to be afraid of.' And they kept at it and said many such things, but it was no use. Myrsina did not show herself. And so they sat at the table and ate their fill and then they went to bed.

And the youngest one said, 'Tomorrow I won't be going along with you. I'll stay here and I will hide, and I shall find out who it is that comes and does all this for us.'

And so, when God made it light again, they all got up and left, except for the youngest one who stayed behind and hid himself behind the door.

Upon which Myrsina came down to busy herself the way she knew how. And as she was about to begin, the youngest month grabbed hold of her by the hem of her skirt and said, 'Well, well, well. So is it you, young miss, who is doing us this kindness and says nothing, but just sits in hiding? Have no fear. We'll keep you as our very own sister. This thing we were asking for from heaven, we've found it here on earth.'

And so Myrsina took courage and she recounted how her sisters had abandoned her and how she'd found herself inside the house. And then she started busying herself with all the chores, just as was her wont. She tidied up the house, she cooked and she got everything arranged nicely, like a proper homebody.

Late that evening, when the months arrived home and saw Myrsina they were glad as glad can be. Such was their joy they didn't quite know how to give vent to it. Then they sat themselves and had their meal and went to sleep like the good brothers they were.

The following day they were up in a trice, and they said to Myrsina, 'Sister dear, make yourself busy as you know best, and you'll see in the evening what kind of brothers we are.'

And with that they were off.

So then Myrsina did all the chores just as she knew how and, as it grew dark, she stepped outside the house and sat waiting for her brothers to get back. She didn't have long to wait, for in a short while there they were, coming home and greeting her joyously.

'Well met, little sister!'

'Welcome back, brothers.'

'What was your day like today?'

'Fine, and what about yours?'

'Ours? Don't you ask about us. If you've had a good day, so have we.'

'So then step inside; don't just stand there. You must be very tired, and the table is all set.'

'It's the truth, Myrsina; you speak well. Let's eat because we're truly famished today.'

And so they went inside and sat themselves at the table. And when they'd had their fill, you should have witnessed the scene! One presented Myrsina with gold earrings and another gave her a gown made from golden cloth embroidered with the sky and its luminaries. Another two gave her gowns embroidered with the earth with its blooms and the sea with its fishes; others brought her as presents other wondrous things, which would sound like fairy tales if one were to hear of them. And so it went, and Myrsina spent her time with the months, with each day more lovely than the one that came before.

Myrsina's sisters, however, were fit to burst with envy when they found out that Myrsina was alive and hale and hearty, and they resolved to poison her. Without further ado they baked her a poisoned cake and came to find her. It was just after the months had left for the day. Thud, thud; they knocked on the door.

'Who is it?' Myrsina sang out from within.

'Fie, Myrsina! Have you forgotten us so quickly? Open up for us; it's your sisters. We were at our wits' end looking for you all over the hills!'

'Bless my heart; it's my sisters,' said Myrsina, and promptly let them in, hugged them tight and burst into tears.

And they said to her, 'Why, whatever's the matter Myrsina? We rushed home, grabbed the mattock and flew back to find you. We looked for you here, we looked for you there, but no trace of Myrsina anywhere! Then we thought: When Myrsina was left all alone she got frightened, and somebody must have passed by and so she went along to some village or other... and to cut a long story short, Myrsina dear, eventually we were told that here you were, so here we are too. We've come to see you, but we can see you're doing well, little sister!'

'Well, what can I say? I'm well. No, more than just well.'

'We can see that for ourselves; now see to it that you don't budge from here, seeing they're so fond of you. Now, we'll be on our way.'

'Why don't you stay a while?'

'No, no, we're in a bit of hurry. Another time; farewell Myrsina.'

'God bless.'

'And we'll be coming round every so often to see you... But hang on a minute now, we almost forgot: here you are; here's a cake for you—it's one of the batch we baked as an offering for the repose of our late mother's soul. Eat it and pray that she be forgiven her sins.'

And Myrsina took it. And when they had left she cut a little portion for the little doggy that she kept as a pet. And before long the poor thing dropped dead. And so Myrsina realized the cake was poisoned, and that her sisters meant to poison her, and she didn't eat any. She shoved it in the oven and it burnt to a cinder.

Then several days went by and Myrsina's sisters found out that Myrsina had not been poisoned. They procured a poisoned ring and went again to see Myrsina. They knocked on the door but Myrsina wouldn't open.

So then they said, 'Open up Myrsina, there's something we have to tell you. Here, we brought you a ring that was our mother's, because you were still a little child when she died, and didn't know what was happening. Our mother, as she lay expiring and her spirit was struggling for release, said, "Here, I charge you with this ring. Give it to Myrsina when she's grown-up." And we wouldn't want to disobey her wishes and risk retribution, so now that you've grown up, here you are, take your ring.'

So Myrsina opened the window and took the ring. But the moment she put it on she was struck down as though dead.

In the evening the months returned home and the moment they set their eyes on Myrsina lying as though dead they began wailing and the echoes came from all around the slopes. After three days they took her and dressed her in cloth of gold and placed her in a casket made of gold and they kept her in the house.

A while had passed and a young prince came by. On beholding the casket he was beguiled by it and asked the lads for it. To start with, they didn't want to part with it. But after he begged and entreated them they gave in and let him have it. But they warned the prince that he was never ever to open it. And the young prince took the casket and brought it to his palace.

And one day he fell sick and was close to dying of his illness. Then he turned to his mother and said, 'Mother, I shall die and I won't have known what the casket holds. Bring it to me that I may open it. But all of you need to step out of the room.'

So, when everybody had left, he opened the casket and what do you think he saw? Myrsina dressed all in gold, and so ravishing was she that, even though dead, she looked like an angel. So the prince was struck with wonder.

When he came to and saw the ring that Myrsina had on, he said, 'Let me take a look at this ring. Is there any writing on it? It might tell me the name of the poor thing who's wearing it.'

And the moment he removed the ring, Myrsina came back to life and sprang out of the casket.

She began to speak and asked, 'Where am I? Who brought me here? Ah! This is not my home. Where are you, my brothers?'

'I am your brother now,' said the prince, 'and you are in the king's palace.'

And then he told her the whole story: how he had brought her from the months, along with her casket, and how she had lain dead inside it and revived when he removed the ring.

Then Myrsina recalled her sisters and she said, 'Oh! My prince. This here ring... throw it into the sea for it is poisoned and bewitched. My sisters brought it to me and the moment I put it on I was poisoned and so it happened that I was left the way you found me.'

Then the prince had Myrsina recount her entire story. And on hearing it he was angered sorely and said, 'Those sisters of yours... even if they are at the ends of the world, I'll find them, just you see, and I know what I'll do to them, for...'

'Don't, my prince, long may you live,' said Myrsina.

'Let them be; don't harm them. Let them get what's coming to them directly from God.'

And then the prince grew calm. And presently, when he had recovered from his sickness, he married Myrsina forthwith, and they lived together in gladness.

But when her sisters found out again that Myrsina was alive and had married the prince, they were sick with envy. And they went to the palace to poison her. They went inside and asked some fellow, 'Where is the princess, Myrsina? We are sisters to her and have come to visit.'

'Just wait a moment,' said the man, 'I'll ask inside, for without the prince's leave nobody can see Myrsina.'

And then he went inside and told the prince: 'My prince, there are two young misses outside and they tell me they are sisters to Princess Myrsina and want to visit. Do they have your leave?'

Then the prince said to one of his entourage, 'Quick! Get those girls, take them and dispose of them as you know best. Because they are here to poison our princess, our sweet Myrsina.'

So they caught the two sisters, but I know not what they did with them. The one thing I do know is that they didn't show their faces ever again, and they were never heard of anywhere else. And so Myrsina and the prince lived on and reigned well, and all everybody had to say of Myrsina was how exquisite she was and how kind were her deeds.

I too went to the palace and got to see Myrsina. And

as I took my leave she gave me a string of florins and then I was on my way home. And as I was passing outside Melachro's house, what do you know, her dog came out and started chasing after me. Then, so that I might escape the dog, I tossed the florins at it, and the dog grabbed them and took off. So when it's daybreak once again, get hold of a hoop and go toss it at Melachro's dog, and it'll give up the coins for you to keep.

The King's Apple Tree

Spun scarlet yarn,
Spun around the spinning wheel,
Kick the treadle, make it whirl,
Let the fairy tale unfurl.

The beginning of the tale
and a very good evening to you:

Once there was a king and in his orchard he had an apple tree that yielded lush red apples, but no matter, he didn't get to eat any of them. The day would come to harvest them and there were none to be had.

One evening his eldest son stood guard at the orchard to catch the thief. At midnight he heard an ogre coming along, wheezing. Struck with fear the boy snuffed out his lamp and hid away.

The following morning:

'How did it go?' his father asked.

'What can I tell you?' he replied. 'At night an ogre came and ate up all the apples.'

The second year the middle son kept guard, but the same thing happened to him.

The third year it was the youngest one's turn. Close to midnight, before cockcrow, he heard the ogre approaching. He also snuffed out his lamp and he took up his bow. When the ogre was close to the apple tree and made to climb up, he loosed an arrow and the ogre was left wounded and bleeding.

The son kept watch till daybreak and then went off to tell his brothers.

They bestirred themselves and all three followed along the trail left by the bleeding ogre. They came to a well and heard the ogre groaning from its depths.

So the youngest said to his brothers, 'I'll tie myself to a line and you can ease me down and then, when I pull on the rope, you'll pull me up.'

'Fine,' they said.

They secured a rope round him and let him down.

So he went down and found the ogre lying at the bottom, groaning. He gave it a blow with the bow and killed it dead.

He looked around him and saw a lass, fresh like cool spring water, close to the ogre.

'For God's sake,' said she to him, 'lend me a hand and deliver me!'

'Have no fear,' said he to her.

He tied the rope around her, and his brothers drew her up.

When they saw her and found out that the ogre had been slain they said, 'Let's leave him there, and let's say it was us that dispatched the ogre.' And so they left him down there and went to their father straight away.

'We killed the ogre,' they said. 'Here, we brought you this lass.'

'Where is your younger brother?' he asked them.

'We haven't a clue,' they said.

When the king saw the girl, he brought her into the palace and commanded that she be well looked after. The lass would neither laugh nor speak; she just sat there, huddled up.

Well, so let's get back to the boy:

When he saw that he had been left at the bottom of the well, what was there for him to do? The lass had surmised that his brothers would be abandoning him there, and she had given him three walnuts, which held three gowns, and she had said, 'When you're left alone in here, two rams will appear, a white one and a black one, and they'll be frisking and gambolling around you. Now see that you catch the white one, and once you've got hold of it you'll be just fine, but if you catch the black one, woe betide you.'

A little later he saw the two rams, lunged to catch the white one, but couldn't: he caught the black one. On getting his hands on it he found himself directly in the netherworld.

What to do now? He set forth and went on and on, and he came to a wizened crone.

'Hey, Granny,' he said, 'would you give me a sip of water to drink?'

'Alas, my boy, we've no water here at all. There's an ogre, and every year it devours one of us, and only then does it let us have a little water. Tomorrow he'll eat the king's daughter.'

And he, on hearing this:

'So,' he said, 'where is the ogre?'

'See, right there,' she said.

So he headed for where they were keeping the princess for the ogre to devour.

'Shush,' he said to her, 'and I shall save you. I shall take a nap and when it comes, you wake me up.'

Before long he heard the ogre wheezing and drawing near.

'Ach,' it said, 'this year they brought me two to eat, not one.'

When it came close the young lad took up his bow and felled the ogre. Then he went to it, took out his knife and cut off all of its seven tongues and put them in his bag. As he started on his way again, behind him the princess placed a sign on him. He went to the crone. Ere long, the blood had merged with the water. People came in a rush to get water, but they saw the king's daughter coming also.

'Don't take any of this water as it is mixed with blood,' she said. 'The ogre has been killed by a brave fighter.'

The king sent out his heralds:

'Whoever killed the ogre must come forward and I will give him my daughter's hand in marriage.'

Several days passed and a shepherd turned up with

his crook and said he was the one who had killed the ogre. The king made him his son-in-law and invited everybody to join in the festivities, men and women alike. They should even bring their cats along and not a soul should be left that didn't turn up. And he enjoined his servants: 'Anybody that filches any bread or viands is to be brought before me.'

An old granny put a hunk of bread in her pocket as she was munching. So the king's servants brought her to the king.

'You,' said the king to her, 'what will you do with that bread that you hid in your pocket?'

'Hear me, my king and master. I have this lad at home, and though I beseeched him to come, he didn't wish to. That's why I took the bread, so as to give it to him.'

'Go back then, and bid him come.'

The old woman went off and came back with the lad.

And as they were sitting and eating, the shepherd came along with his crook.

'All rise,' he said.

Everybody stood up on their two legs.

'What are you all getting up for?' said the lad to them.

'Hush,' they said, 'lest he hear you. Just you stand up too, and on the double; he's the one that slew the ogre.'

'Has he the look of somebody that could slay an ogre? If it were he that slew it... I've got a sack at the old woman's house and if he can bring it to me then I'll believe that he slew the ogre.'

So the shepherd went to fetch it but he couldn't get it to budge.

When the princess saw him, she knew the sign that she'd put on him.

'*He's* the one,' she said. 'He's the one that killed the ogre.'

They caught the shepherd and cut him to pieces for having hoodwinked them. Then the lad brought his sack and took out the tongues one by one, all seven of them, and showed them to everyone. Then they feasted joyfully and celebrated, and the king did his utmost to get him married to his daughter, but the lad didn't want to for his thoughts were on the girl he'd rescued from the well.

There came a day when he was sad and doleful, and he took his bow and went outside into the orchards. He saw a large tree with a serpent slithering up to an eagle's nest at the top. And he heard the little eaglets chirping—chirp, chirp. He looked up and realized the serpent was going to eat the little eaglets. He let go an arrow and killed the serpent. Then he lay down and fell asleep under the tree.

A while later the mother and the father of the eaglets came back. When they saw him:

'Ah, so it's you,' they said, 'that eats up our babies each year?'

They lunged at him in order to gouge out his eyes.

'Chirp, chirp,' their fledglings twittered. 'He is the one,' they said, 'that saved us!'

Then they spread their wings to give him shade so that he would sleep comfortably. When he woke up:

'So what would you like us to do for you in return for your kindness? It's been ever so many years and we hadn't managed to raise our nestlings, and now you've dispatched our foe.'

'There's nothing that I want from you except that you bring me to the world above.'

'We can do that,' they said, 'but we shall need food.'

'What will that be?'

'We will need forty sheep and forty skins of water.'

'Fine,' he said.

So he went to the king:

'Give me,' he said, 'forty skins of water and forty sheep.'

'Immediately,' said the king.

He gave the lad forty sheep and forty skins of water. The lad put them on the eagles and mounted one himself.

As they flew the eagles would screech 'cra' (*kréas* is Greek for meat) and he'd feed them meat. They would cry 'na' (*neró* is Greek for water) and he'd give them water. They brought him close to the world above but then the meat was all finished. And they screeched, and for his yearning to get to the world above he cut off a piece of his own shank and gave it to them. Realizing what it was they didn't eat it. They brought him up to the world above.

'Now, march ahead,' they said, 'so we can see you at it.'

He made as if to walk, but he was limping. They put the flesh back onto his shank, and he walked properly.

Then he went to the city, to a tailor:

'Take me on,' he said, 'as your apprentice—for my daily bread, and keep me in your shop.'

The tailor took him in, and kept him as help.

Meanwhile, the king, his father, was importuning himself on the young beauty, the princess, that she take him for her husband.

After much ado, she said to him, 'When you get me a gown that has the sun and the moon and the sky with all its stars I'll marry you.'

'Fine,' said the king.

So the king called for the tailor, and said to him, 'Tomorrow, at five o'clock, I need a gown that has the sky with its stars and the sun and the moon. If not, it'll be off with your head.'

The tailor heard this and swooned. He went back to his shop and prepared himself to die. What could he do, poor man? For to make the gown was entirely out of the question.

'What's the matter, master? Why so pensive?' said his apprentice.

'That's no business of yours,' he replied. 'It isn't your affair.'

'Do tell me,' he said, 'and maybe I can do something about it.'

'Oh, my lad,' he said, 'I'm lost. The king asked me to make a gown with the sky and its stars.'

'Have no fear,' he said. 'I'll get it made this very evening. Bring me,' he said, 'nine ells of stuff, four quarts of schnapps and four pecks of walnuts.'

Throughout the night he did nothing else but crack walnuts and eat them and drink schnapps. The tailor spied on him through a chink, but could see not a thing.

'Woe is me,' he said. 'Is the boy going to get anything done? Woe is me that I put my trust in him.'

Come morning, the tailor knocked at his door.

'Still asleep?' he said. 'Get up, you sleepyhead. It's time to take the gown to the king and you are acting as though nothing's amiss.'

'Ach,' he said, 'you didn't let me sleep at all, all night. There I was, struggling until dawn; I only got to sleep just now.'

The tailor opened the door wide and beheld the gown. The lad had taken it out, all finished, from the walnut given to him by the lass he had brought out of the well. So the tailor took it directly to the king and the king brought it directly to the lass.

'Good,' she said. 'Get me one more gown with the sea and its fishes.'

So he called for the tailor once more and told him, and he told the apprentice, and once again brought him the walnuts and the schnapps. Again, until dawn the apprentice kept eating and drinking. When it was close to morning, he handed the gown from one of the walnuts to the tailor, who took it to the lass.

'Good,' she said, 'but I want one more now, with the earth and its flowers.'

The following day the lad produced it again, and the tailor brought it over.

'Good,' said the lass to the king. 'Get the master who made it. I want to have a look at him.'

The tailor went to the king and the lass asked him, 'Did you make this by yourself or did somebody else have a hand in it?'

Then the tailor became frightened and told the truth—how his apprentice had made them all.

The king then called for the apprentice and found him to be his son! They embraced and remained embracing one another for some good while.

'It's you, my son,' he said, 'that should have her for your wife.'

They celebrated and feasted for days and days and, after that, the king abdicated and handed him his throne, and made him king, his youngest son.

His brothers were left hangdog, sorely mortified.

I was also there and doing my rounds. They gave me a big bone from the kitchens, and I took it with me and was on my way to come here. I meant to get across the ford, and the frogs were croaking 'vrak, vrak' and it seemed to me that it was some Turks, saying to me 'brak, brak' (*drop it, drop it*). I got scared and tossed it away. And it hit Koutsargyris (lame Argyris) right on his foot and he's had this limp ever since, and if you don't believe me, you just take a look at him and see.

Maroula

To get started with our fairy tale,
first we bid you gentlefolk a very good evening.

Once upon a time there was a woman who had no children and each and every day she beseeched God that He might grant her a child.

One morning, as she stood at the window, she turned to the sun and addressed him.

'Oh my sun, my good sir sun, grant me a child, and when it gets to be twelve years of age you can come and fetch it away.'

The sun heeded her entreaties and gave her a baby girl, as beautiful as the morning star. The woman called her Maroula and was filled with joy at having had a child.

As Maroula grew, she became ever more beautiful, until she turned twelve.

One day when she went to the spring to fetch water, the sun saw her, turned himself into a lad, approached her and said, 'Tell your mother, when will she give me what she promised me?'

'Um, and who might you be?' Maroula asked the lad.

And he replied, 'You tell her what I told you and she will know who it be.'

'Alright, I'll tell her,' said Maroula.

She took up her jar, went back home and said to her mother, 'Mother, a lad came to me at the spring where I was, but what a lad! So handsome was he that he shone like the sun. That face of his! And he asked when you would give him what you promised him. I asked him who he might be and he said you'd know who it is.'

And her mother heaved a sigh, and said to her, 'My girl, I know this lad. Just you tell him, if he finds you again, that you forgot to tell me.'

The following day the girl again went for water, and the sun came down and asked her, 'Did you ask your mother what I told you?'

'I forgot to tell her,' said she.

Then the sun gave her a golden apple and said to her, 'There, take this apple and put it in your bosom and, in the evening, when your mother undresses you for bed, the apple will fall out, and you will remember and tell her.'

Then Maroula went back home all fired up with joy, and said to her mother, 'That there lad who told me to tell you about the promise you'd made him, and asked when you'd give it to him, he found me again and gave me this apple, and asked me to put it in my bosom so that in the evening, as you undressed me for bed, it would fall out and I'd remember to tell you.'

'When he finds it, let him take it!' said her mother and made a mental note not to send the girl out for water any more.

She didn't send Maroula to fetch water for quite some while, but then she grew bold and sent her. But when the sun saw her, he turned again into a lad and came down and asked Maroula what her mother had said about the promise she had made him.

'Oh,' said Maroula. 'When you find it,' she said, 'let you take it.'

So the sun took Maroula by the hand and carried her away to his palace which, at the front, had a lovely garden.

All day long the sun was away and Maroula was left in the garden to play, and he would return to his palace in the evening. But poor Maroula, though she had all kinds of delicacies and finery at the sun's palace, would pine for her mother, and all day long she sat in the garden and wept and said:

Just as my mother's poor heart grows cold and withers,
Thus let the sun's garden grow cold and waste!
Get you felled, my tree, get you felled!

And she set her nails to her cheeks and tore at them. And the vegetables in the garden wilted and the trees were felled, for Maroula's weeping.

The sun returned in the evening and found Maroula with eyes all swollen and cheeks torn to shreds.

'Who did this to you, my Maroula?'

'The neighbour's cockerel came along and fought with ours, so I tried to part them and they scratched me.'

The following day Maroula sat in the garden, and began weeping once more, and tearing at her cheeks and saying:

Just as my mother's poor heart grows cold and withers,
Thus let the sun's garden grow cold and waste!
Get you felled, my tree, get you felled!

And the vegetables wilted and the trees were felled.

The sun returned in the evening and, again, found her with her cheeks all torn up.

'Why, who got you like this again, my Maroula?'

'The neighbour's tomcat came along and had a fight with ours. I tried to separate them and they scratched me.'

The following morning, once again Maroula went into the garden and when she sat down her mind went to her mother, and she tore at her cheeks till they were bloody again, and she wept and said:

Just as my mother's poor heart grows cold and withers,
Thus let the sun's garden grow cold and waste!
Get you felled, my tree, get you felled!

And so all the vegetables wilted and all the trees were felled and the garden was left dry as dust and blighted.

The sun came in the evening and saw Maroula all bloodied.

'Who got you like this again, my Maroula?'

'I walked by a rose bush,' said Maroula to him, 'and it tore at me with its thorns.'

But the following morning, as he came out, the sun thought, 'Shouldn't I have a look and see what Maroula is doing in the garden?' So he turned round and what do you think he saw? Maroula weeping and tearing at her cheeks.

He approached her and said, 'Why are you crying, my Maroula? Are you sad, perhaps, to be here?'

'No,' she said, 'I am not sad.'

'So then, why are you crying? Would you be wanting to return to your mother?'

'Yes, I want to go back to my mother!' said Maroula.

'Well, if you want to go back to her,' said the sun, 'then I'll send you to her.'

So he took her by the hand and brought her to the garden's edge and called out, 'Lions, my little lions!'

The lions bestirred themselves and headed towards him.

'What is your wish, master?' they said to him.

'Will you take Maroula to her mother?'

'Yes, we'll take her.'

'And what will you eat along the way if you feel hungry, and what will you drink if you feel thirsty?'

'We'll eat of her flesh and drink of her blood.'

'Be gone quickly,' said the sun. 'You won't do.'

Then he called out again: 'Foxes, my little foxes!'

The foxes bestirred themselves and headed towards him.

'What is your wish, master?' they said to him.

'Will you take Maroula to her mother?'

'Yes, we'll take her.'

'And what will you eat along the way if you feel hungry, and what will you drink if you feel thirsty?'

'We'll eat of her flesh and drink of her blood.'

'Be gone quickly. Away with you,' said the sun, and then he called out once more: 'Stags, my little stags!'

The stags bestirred themselves and headed to him briskly.

'Will you take Maroula to her mother?'

'Yes, we'll take her.'

'And what will you eat along the way when you feel hungry, and what will you drink when you feel thirsty?'

'Succulent green grass and clear spring water.'

'With my blessing,' said the sun to them, and he decked Maroula out with florins and lifted her up on to the antlers of one of them, and sent her to her mother.

On and on they went, and at some point the stag felt hungry. He came to a cypress and said, 'Bend down, O cypress, that I may perch Maroula on you!'

The cypress bent itself and Maroula perched upon it.

'Now,' said the stag, 'I shall go and graze for a little while, and then I'll come back to fetch you. Mind you, don't you call me, save only if you really have need of me; otherwise just let me graze.'

'Alright', said Maroula, 'you go on now.'

Beneath the cypress was a well, and close by an ogress lived together with her three daughters, and she bid one of them to fetch water from the well. As the daughter stooped to throw the pail into the well, she beheld Maroula's face mirrored in the water and imagined that it was her own. She threw the pail away and went home a-dancing.

'Did you bring me the water?' her mother asked her.

'Such a maiden as am I, and you bid me fetch you water?'

Her mother was dumbstruck. She sent the second one to the well, but she also, on seeing Maroula's face reflected in the water, took it for her own. She tossed the pail aside and went skipping back to her mother.

'Such a maiden as am I, and you bid me fetch you water?'

So then she sent her third daughter to the well, but the same thing happened all over again.

So their mother went to the well herself. She stooped, gazed into the water and saw Maroula's face. She looked up and saw the girl herself, and she was in stitches with laughter.

'Ah, you silly thing,' said the ogress to her, 'so it was you that my daughters saw in the water and came back home all in a tizzy, and it's for your sake I cut short my kneading! You get down now so I can gobble you up!'

'Well and good, but first you finish your kneading,' said Maroula to her, 'and then you can come and gobble me up.'

The ogress rushed back home, finished up her kneading in two shakes and rushed back to Maroula.

'I've finished kneading,' she told her. 'Now get you down so I can gobble you up.'

'Fie, go form your loaves first,' Maroula said to her, 'and then you come back.'

The ogress sped off, formed the loaves and sped back.

'I've formed the loaves,' she said to Maroula. 'Now get you down that I may gobble you up.'

'Yes, but first you need to fire the oven, and then you can come back and eat me.'

The ogress went to fire the oven and then returned.

'I've fired the oven,' she said. 'Get you down now so I can gobble you up.'

'Well, bake the loaves first lest the oven grow cold on you,' said Maroula, 'and then you can come back and eat me up.'

The ogress went away to bake her loaves, and Maroula let out a cry.

'Stag, little stag!'

The stag heard and came to her a-running.

'Quick!' said Maroula. 'The ogress has come to eat me up.'

And then the little stag said, 'Bend down, cypress, so I can carry Maroula away!'

The tree bent low and the stag carried Maroula away, breaking into a brisk trot.

Along the way they happened on a little mouse, and

the stag said to it, 'Little mouse, if you meet an ogress on your way, and she asks you whether you've seen us, tell her lots and lots of words, so you'll make her tarry, lest she catch up with us.'

A little later there came the ogress, and she said to the mouse, 'Hey, little mouse, did you happen to meet a maiden with a stag?'

The little mouse said to her, 'I've just found myself a nice big tuft of wool right here.'

The ogress said to the mouse, 'I'm talking of one thing; you're talking of another. Have you seen a maiden with a stag?'

'Just a moment, for as long as I need to card it!' said the little mouse.

'I'm talking of one thing,' said the ogress, 'and you're talking of another. Have you seen a maiden with a stag?'

'Just a moment, for as long as I need to spin it!' said the little mouse.

'I'm talking of one thing; you're talking of another. Have you seen a maiden with a stag?'

'Just a moment, for as long as I need to weave it!' said the little mouse.

'I'm talking of one thing; you're talking of another. Haven't you seen a maiden with a stag?'

'Yes, I've seen her; indeed I have,' said the little mouse. 'Now you run along so as you may catch up with her.'

As the stag was speeding on and getting closer to Maroula's mother's house, the dog sensed Maroula approaching and started baying: 'Woof, woof! Here's

Maroula coming; here's Maroula coming.' And Maroula's mother said, 'Bad dog, be off with you! Do you mean to make me explode in a fit of grief?'

Then the tomcat on the roof tiles sensed Maroula's approach and wailed 'miaow, miaow! Here's Maroula coming,' and her mother said, 'Fie, bad tom! Do you mean to make me explode in a fit of grief?'

Then the cockerel sensed Maroula, and crowed: 'cock-a-doodle! cock-a-doodle! Here's Maroula coming,' and her mother said, 'You naughty, naughty cockerel! Do you mean to make me explode in a fit of grief and sorrow?'

But as the stag was getting ever so close to the house, so was the ogress; and as the stag had almost entered through the front door, the ogress managed to grab hold of its tail.

'My poor tail, my poor tail!' squealed the stag.

When it had gained the house, Maroula's mother stood up and welcomed it. 'Welcome, welcome, and since you've brought me back my beloved darling, Maroula, I'll make up for your little tufted tail.' And she picked up a ball of cotton wool and put the stag's tail back on.

And ever since then she's lived with her little girl, and they've been happy and full of joy, and as for us, we've been even better still.

Poppies

Once there was an old woman and she had a daughter, and she would send her out to gather greens.

On a day in May, when the fields were full of flowers and the trees were budding with new leaves, the girl went into a meadow and, instead of gathering greens, she picked poppies! And she had a needle too, and she stitched them onto her pinafore.

As she decked herself from head to toe, my darling, the three Fates came by and, when they beheld her, they laughed. Even the youngest laughed, who'd never laughed before.

So the Fates said to her, 'Seeing that you made our sister laugh too, what shall we grant you?'

'Those flowers that you are wearing... may they become sparkling diamonds,' said the first. The second one said, 'May you be the fairest in the world and, when you speak, may blooms and roses drop from your mouth.'

And the third one, the youngest, said, 'You, who made me laugh, the king will come by at this hour and he'll take you as his wife. He'll lose his head on beholding you.'

The girl was all changed, and full of glamour. Finally, my darling, there was the king coming by at that moment and, on beholding her, his eyes were struck with wonder, and he was dumbfounded at her sheer loveliness.

He said to her, 'Are you human or a sprite?'

'Human,' she said.

And then he said, 'Come close to me,' and he whisked her up onto his steed, and he took her to his mother.

On seeing her, his mother said, 'My boy, my boy, what is this? Such a thing, it must be a sprite!'

'No, my mother,' he says, 'it's a woman. Don't you worry.'

To cut a long story short, there were no two ways about it: he had to have her as his wife, and that he did! They lived together contentedly.

One fine day, as they were in their room and she was combing his hair, she got to giggling. The king said to her. 'What are you laughing at?'

'Ah, my dear,' she said, 'what can I tell you? I'm laughing because your beard seemed to me just like the sweeping brush in our palace.'

'God Almighty!' exclaimed the king at once. 'Is this how low I've fallen in your eyes?'

He convened his privy council of twelve to see what their ruling would be. And they advised him to have her put to death.

So then the Fates, who had pronounced her destiny, realized what was afoot.

'Just see,' they said, 'that brainless chit of a girl, what she's gone and done!' And they wrought three frigates and made themselves turn into three handsome young lads, and went to that place. And they dropped anchor.

'Three royal ships are here, three royal vessels!' and everybody rushed out to look at the ships.

The king dressed in his finery and went to receive his guests. So the three men said to him, 'We heard you have our sister here, who we thought was lost.'

'Indeed,' said the king, and he was scared witless.

So he took the youths with him to the palace. A banquet was prepared. They sat down and ate and said, 'We'd like to see our sister.'

So they went to the queen's parlour and said to her, 'You dolt, whatever possessed you to say such a thing to him? Wasn't it enough that we made you a queen, but you had to give such great offence to the king? He has resolved to have you put to death. But seeing that we are the Fates that decreed your destiny for having made our sister laugh… Here, take this little brush that is all diamonds and precious stones and hang it behind the door, and if the king should come in and ask what it is, tell him, "My sovereign, this is the thing I spoke of to you, because that's the kind of article we have in the palace, so that you show how very rich you are." And next time you be more careful, because, silly thing, it's only because you made our sister laugh that we have done this one more favour for you, for the king had resolved to have your head chopped off.'

So they bid her farewell, and the king bid them farewell, and they boarded their frigates and sailed away.

Then the king went back to the palace and visited the queen in her parlour. And as he was about to shut the door he saw this object, so golden it was, that lovely brush, and it was hanging behind the door, and his eyes glinted with a gleam of light.

He said, 'What is this thing?'

'It's what I told you your beard looks like.'

On hearing that he said to himself, 'Ah! I was wrong to want to kill her, poor thing. She didn't mean to belittle me; she meant to do me honour, and I mistook her words.'

And he was filled with love for his wife, and they had a lovely life, and we an even better one.

Neither was I there, nor should you believe it.

Lord Frumenty

Once upon a time there was a king and he had a daughter. There were many suitors asking for her hand, but she would have none of them, because none were to her liking. So she came up with the idea of making herself a man of her own.

She got hold of six pounds of almonds and six pounds of sugar and six pounds of wheatgerm semolina, pounded the almonds thoroughly and kneaded everything together, the sugar, the almonds and the semolina, and set about shaping a man, who she propped up before the icons of the protector saints of the house. And she began praying continually and performing innumerable prostrations. Forty days and forty nights she kept beseeching God, and on the fortieth day God quickened him to life, and they called him by the names of Lord Frumence and Lord Frumenty.

He was unbelievably good-looking and his fame spread to the ends of the world.

A queen in a far-off kingdom heard about Lord Frumence and resolved to go and get him for herself. So she had a golden galley built, with oars of gold, and she voyaged over the high seas to where Lord Frumenty lived.

When she arrived she said to the seamen, 'Whoever stands out for his good looks... grab him and bring him to my galley.'

When people heard that a golden galley had sailed in they all went to have a look, and so too did Lord Frumenty.

The moment the seamen saw him they knew who he was, and directly they grabbed hold of him and took him aboard the galley!

That evening the princess was waiting for Frumenty to turn up, and she waited and waited... but to no avail! She asked this fellow and that, and was told that a queen had grabbed hold of him and spirited him away.

What to do then? What to do?

She went and had three pairs of iron brogues made and set out on the road to seek him.

On and on she marched and marched, and she left the world far behind her and went and found the moon's mother.

'Good morrow, good mother.'

'Well met, my girl. How now, young lass? What fetches you to these parts?'

'My fortune has brought me here. Would you by chance have seen Lord Frumence anywhere, my Lord Frumenty?'

'Where, my lass? Why, I haven't ever heard this name before. But wait a bit until my lad gets back in the evening. He makes his rounds all over the world and might have seen him somewhere.'

That evening, when the moon came back home, she said to him, 'My child, this damsel is asking you to tell her whether there's any place you might have seen Lord Frumence, her Lord Frumenty.'

'Where? I haven't seen him, my lass. It's the first I hear this name. Go ask the sun. He might have seen him, for he roams around the world far more than do I.'

That night she slept there, and in the morning they handed her an almond saying to her, 'When you are beset by need, crack it open.'

The princess took the almond and was on her way.

On she goes and on she goes, and she wore down her first pair of brogues just as she reached the sun's mother.

'Good morrow, good mother.'

'Well met, my girl. How now, young lass? What fetches you to these parts?'

'My fortune has brought me here. Would you by chance have seen Lord Frumence, my Lord Frumenty?'

'Where, my lass? I haven't seen him. Just wait a while until my lad returns in the evening; he might have seen him, for he goes about a lot around the world.'

The sun came home in the evening, and the princess knelt down before him and said to him, 'My sun, my lord sun, who circles around the world, might you have seen Lord Frumence, my Lord Frumenty?'

'Where? I haven't seen him. Why don't you ask the stars that are so many in number? One of them might have seen him.'

That night she slept there, and in the morning they handed her a walnut and said to her, 'When you are beset by need, crack it open.'

Then they showed her the way and she took her leave of them and was gone.

On she goes and on she goes, and she had worn down another pair of brogues by the time she reached the mother of the stars.

'Good morrow, good mother.'

'Well met, my girl. How now, young lass? What fetches you to these parts?'

'My fortune has brought me here. Would you by chance have seen Lord Frumence, my Lord Frumenty?'

'Where, my lass? I haven't seen him. Just wait a while though, until my brood get back in the evening. One of them might have seen him.'

Her children came home in the evening and she asked them, 'Have you seen Lord Frumence, my Lord Frumenty?'

'No, we haven't seen him,' said the stars.

But a smallish one piped up and said, 'I have seen him.'

'Where did you see him?'

'At them bleached houses, hostelries—the crane, the birdy, saw it too—that's where the queen keeps him and watches over him, lest they take him from her.'[2]

That night she slept there. When it was morning they showed her the way, handed her a filbert and said to her, 'When you are beset by need, crack it open.'

On she goes and on she goes, and she got to where Lord Frumence was sojourning.

She went to the palace in the guise of a beggarwoman, and there she saw Lord Frumence, but said not a word.

They had lots of geese at the palace. She went to the serving maids and said to them, 'Couldn't you let me bide over there where you keep the geese?'

The serving maids went to the queen and said to her, 'Ma'am queen, there's a beggarwoman out there and she's asking us to let her sit by the geese. What are we to do?'

'Let her,' said the queen.

And there they let her stay. That's where she slept that night.

Next morning, when she had arisen, she cracked the almond and out came a spinning wheel made of gold,

---

[2] Aesop, in his fable 'Peacock and Crane', writes of the crane, 'Coming close to the stars I speak with them, for I soar high up in the heavens.'

with a golden crank, spinning out spools of gold. The servants saw and ran to the queen to tell her all about it.

When the queen heard, she said, 'Bestir yourselves. Bid her to let us have it. What need has she of it?'

The serving maids went to her and said, 'Our mistress the queen asks might you give us the golden spinning wheel and its crank? What need have you of it?'

'All right, you can take it. Just let me have Lord Frumence for a night.'

The serving maids went and told the queen.

'Indeed, why not let her have him!' said the queen. 'Where's the harm in that?'

So that evening, after they had eaten, the queen gave Lord Frumence to drink a potion that had sleep in it. The moment he swallowed a draught of it he fell asleep, and the serving maids lifted him in their arms and brought him to the beggarwoman and took away the golden spinning wheel and the crank.

When the serving maids had gone, the princess started addressing Lord Frumence thus: 'Why will you not awaken? Is it not I who made you? I who ground the almonds, the sugar and the semolina and kneaded them to a paste? Who wore through three pairs of iron brogues to come and find you, and now will you not speak to me? Have you no pity for me, my eyes and light of my eyes?'

That is what the princess kept saying all night long, but Frumenty remained in deep sleep and there was no waking him!

The following morning the serving maids came and took Lord Frumence away, and the queen gave him another potion to drink and he woke up.

Once the servants had gone, the princess cracked the walnut and out sprang a golden hen with golden chicks.

The servants saw the golden hen with her golden chicks and hurried to the queen to tell her.

'Run along,' said the queen. 'Bid her give them to us. What need has she of them? And if she tells you we should let her have Lord Frumenty, we shall. What harm will come of it? What harm came of it the evening we let her spend with him?'

The serving maids went to her and said, 'How about you give us the golden hen with the golden chicks? What need have you of them?'

'If you let me have Lord Frumenty for one more night...'

'You can have him,' said the serving maids.

So once again the queen gave Lord Frumence some sleep to drink, and the moment he swooned the servants lifted him up in their arms, carried him to the beggarwoman and came away with the golden hen and the golden chicks.

The moment they left her the princess started telling her woes once more as she had done on the first evening, but there was no waking Lord Frumence! And in the morning the servants returned, took away Lord Frumence again and left.

The beggarwoman then cracked the filbert, and out of it sprang a carnation shrub with gold carnations. When the serving girls saw the golden carnation shrub with the gold carnations, they ran to the queen and told her about it.

'Go to her and tell her to give it to us. What does she want with it? And if again she wants Lord Frumenty, she's welcome to him,' said the queen.

And the serving maids went and told her.

But close by, where the beggarwoman was biding, sat a tailor, and he had been sewing away at night, and he had heard everything the beggarwoman had been saying.

So he went and found Lord Frumence and said to him, 'Beg your pardon, Majesty, I've a question to ask you.'

'Ask away,' said Lord Frumence.

'Where do you sleep at night?'

'Whyever do you ask? At home! Where would I be sleeping?'

'Lord Frumence, I haven't slept a wink these past two nights, because of that beggarwoman you've got with the geese. She sits up all night and says, "Lord Frumence, why do you not awaken? I've gone through three pairs of iron brogues to come and find you and now will you not talk to me?"'

Lord Frumence realized what was amiss, but said nothing.

He went and readied his horse and loaded it with a saddlebag full of florins.

That evening the queen gave him to drink of the draught again, but he didn't drink of it and just feigned sleep.

Presently the servant maids lifted him up in their arms and brought him to the beggarwoman, and they fetched away the golden carnation shrub with the gold carnations.

Then, when the servants had gone and the princess began recounting her woes again, Lord Frumenty rose up, took her in his arms and they mounted the steed at once and away they galloped.

The following morning the servants went to retrieve Lord Frumenty, but he was nowhere to be found! They ran back to the queen in tears with their news. She broke out weeping also, but to what avail?

So then she said, 'I shall also make me a man,' and right away she had her serving maids crack a quantity of almonds, and she mixed them with sugar and semolina and she set herself to perform her prostrations. But rather than prayers, she uttered imprecations and blasphemies, and upon forty days the man spoiled and they had to get rid of him.

The princess with Lord Frumenty went back to their kingdom and they had a lovely life, if not quite the loveliest. I too was there, enjoying a stroll.

Fairies

Fairies, *Neraides* in Greek,[3] inhabit meadows, dells, places where trees and streams abound. These 'gentle ladies' may be espied by those whose guardian spirit is not particularly robust. Ineffably beautiful, with their long, fair hair, they relish revelry and mirth. Often, they capture skilled singers and musicians for the enjoyment of their song and music making. They entice handsome lads too, to go to bed with them, and once one has slept with a fairy there's no going back to ordinary women. This is why it is said of those who are ineffectual with women, that in their youth they must have been in thrall to fairies.

Were anybody to disturb their peace as they sit at table, feasting or amusing themselves, they would wreak

[3] Not to be confused with Nereids, the fifty daughters of marine deity Nereus.

the most appalling retribution. And that is why it is said that if, for no apparent reason, anyone comes to harm all of a sudden, in a field, or a thicket, or a glen, especially round midday, then fairies must have injured them for having trodden upon their repast as they were dining or for spoiling their merriment. This is something everybody knows, and when one chances upon fairies, one ought to hold one's tongue and say only, well under one's breath, 'Milk and honey on your wings!'

In Gortynia in the Peloponnese it is said that wherever there is water flowing forth, there's a fairy dwelling there. It is the reason why, after dark, when one chooses to follow a path beside which there's running water, one ought to speak not lest the fairy steal one's voice. But in some circumstances (this is spoken of by a number of women, for they have seen it) at night the water lies slumbering: what we're saying here is that it just remains stilled, without any movement whatsoever, and at that very moment the fairy is right there with the water. For the fairy to go away and the water to resume its flow, here is what needs be done: one should cast a pebble into the water and promptly the fairy takes flight, so then the water is released to flow afresh.

A fairy is not visible to all and sundry: horses can see her, and they become startled and shy away and choose not to go on the path she trod; dogs too, but only those four-eyed ones, namely the ones with markings atop their brows, the dark ones with light brows, the light ones with dark—all the other ones see her not.

In Galaxidi near Delphoi they still talk about how many years back, before he'd settled down, our friend Thanasis would sleep under haystacks. It was summer, the month for threshing. As he lay drowsing he heard footfalls—prancing, skipping and gambolling—as of dancing, and an angelic singing. He opened his eyes just a crack, peered around and saw several women gathered there, each one lovelier than the next and all a-dancing. Thanasis realized these were fairies, so he propped himself up ever so gently to have a look, for he was dauntless. But the fairies, sensing they'd been noticed, straightaway snatched their scarves, which they'd spread on the haystacks, and vanished like lightning. Then Thanasis thought to himself, 'These ones who come here, clearly they aren't worried that somebody might catch them, so they're bound to be back again.' And he resolved to feign sleep the following noontide and filch the scarf of a certain one he'd set his sights on. For when you take a fairy's scarf she surrenders to you.

Thanasis had done with his chores when he lay down at his favourite spot, just waiting, his eyes half-shut. So tired was he, however, that sleep overwhelmed him. Meantime the fairies did show up and they danced for quite some while, and then, as they were getting ready to go, Thanasis started up from his snoozing. But he wasn't nearly quick enough, for the fairies had disappeared already.

Our worthy fellow was tenacious though and on the morrow he returned there early in the morning without having done any work at all. Presently, out of the blue, there they were: the fairies appeared right at midday and whipped out their scarves and began dancing. Thanasis let them be for a while, that they might grow heedless as they danced. Then he sprang up stealthily and snatched the scarf of the fairy he'd set his heart on. The other fairies grabbed their scarves and fled and only she remained whose scarf had been forfeit—Thanasis' captive. He took her home with him, wedded her and before long they had children too.

The years passed and they had a pretty fair life of it and everybody said how fortunate they were. But suddenly, one morning as she was tidying away some clothes in her husband's chest, the fairy found her scarf. She removed it at once, placed it on her head and vanished like vapour! Thanasis returned home and called after his wife, but she was nowhere to be found. He asked his children and they told him they hadn't seen her since that morning. He was struck to the depths of his heart by grief, that he had lost such an able and lovely helpmeet, so on the third day he dressed in black and got up his children in full mourning too.

A few days later though he saw that his children were properly dressed and combed again, as previously, and he asked them who had told them to put on a fresh change of clothes and who had combed their hair like that. To begin with the children didn't dare to tell him, for that was what their mother had instructed. But after a while, as their father pressed them, they were obliged to own up that their mother came regularly, each morning, to visit them. To cut a long story short, he lay in wait one morning and as the fairy came into the house he took away her scarf again, threw it in the oven and burnt it to a cinder. And that's how he got to keep her with him for good.

Goblins

Goblins, or *kallikantzaroi*, come from below the ground. During the twelve days of Christmas they infest the villages, then they vanish on the eve of Epiphany. All year long they keep chopping with their axes at the tree that holds up the earth in order to fell it. They chop and they chop until just a little remains, no thicker than a sturdy branch, and they say 'Leave it, let's go, and it will topple over on its own.' They return on Epiphany and they find the tree healed, intact, unharmed. And once again they get back to chopping away and they keep coming back and having a go at it afresh, and so on, forever and ever again. It's their way of going about things. On Christmas Eve they turn up from all sorts of places and loiter outside villages, and when day bleeds into night they move in. They are nasty and scheming and vicious and scary, and have ghastly long claws, which they never trim, and with these they scratch people's faces. But there are goblins, too, that cannot harm humans and that is the reason women taunt them and call them names, such as cinder-pads, ashy-kins, pisser-boy and many more such.

Every single goblin is blighted by some disfigurement as, too, are their animals. Some are lame, some blind, some have only one good eye or one leg only to stand on or an ill-shaped mouth, or lopsided features, or their visage is all awry, or they've a withered arm, or they have a pigeon chest, or are hunchbacks or they're marred in other ways. In short, one finds all kinds of blemishes and handicaps afflicting them. And as is their own appearance, so too is that of their clothes: tattered, frayed, ill-fitting, made of sundry mismatched patches. The same goes too for the tack and ornaments they use on their animals.

And their ways and manners, and their gait too, and all their foibles are ludicrous and show them up as incredibly oafish, nothing but clods. For instance, one may be long-shanked, tall as tall can be, but he mounts a puny cockerel and his feet drag on the ground, while another, short as short can be, sits there on a donkey so high up that when he falls off he cannot climb on his mount again, but calls for help; the donkey may trample the shanks of the tall one, who yowls and hurls abuse. Meantime, another one seeks to mount his one-eyed dog, so he clambers and scuffles over them all to get a leg up.

They devour worms, small toads, snakes and other such unclean vermin. And while one is feeding, another relieves himself before him. So the one eating gets furious and starts beating the other. Then there are those others, always getting into squabbles and brawls among themselves for no reason at all.

And whenever they attempt some undertaking or other they cannot bring it to completion, for they are quarrelsome and irresolute, with one saying aye and the other one saying nay. When they set off towards a destination to attend to their affairs, one hurries along, the other dawdles behind. They get into a wrangle while on the road and they never get to where they're headed, or they arrive when it's far too late. That's why they cannot cause people much harm even though it is their most earnest wish to do so.

It is said in Zakynthos that goblins gain entry from chimneys, which is why good housewives set down a colander close by the hearth. Goblins come into a house meaning to do some mischief or other, but on seeing the colander they feel compelled to count its holes, but in counting they lose track of time and, before they know it, it's daybreak, and once the first cock crows they have to make themselves scarce.

In Argos they say that along with male goblins there are also female ones. Male and female goblins try to hoodwink people, leading them to water for them to drown, or to precipices to make them trip and tumble onto the rocks below. They tell of a woman led away by a female goblin who'd come to her in the guise of a neighbour. The goblin had taken her to the seaside, two hours' walk from Argos. And there she would've had her drowned, but the woman realized something was amiss, turned round and came away. As she did so, the female goblin broke into cackles and guffaws, mocking her.

The Fisherman's Child

There once was a fisherman and he had turned fifty and had no children. He spent all day fishing and he would become dead tired.

'Oh!' he'd say, 'I wish I also had a little child to give me a bit of rest!'

There came one day when his toil made him dizzy and he collapsed.

'Oh, dear God,' he said, 'if only I also had a little child!'

A mermaid surfaced out of the sea close to him and said to him, 'What's the matter with you that causes you to groan so?'

'What's the matter with me?' he said. 'I've been trying to get me a child for years and years that it might relieve my weariness, as I struggle and strive all day long.'

'I'll give you a child. When it turns twelve, will you bring it back to me?'

'Alright,' he said, filled with longing and because he reckoned that by the time it was twelve she'd have forgotten.

'Take this apple,' said the mermaid, 'and eat it and next year your wife will bear you a child.'

So, full of yearning, he took it from her and ate it all.

The following year his wife gave birth to a little boy, just as the mermaid had promised. The more the child grew, the more handsome he became. But the father, by dint of his gladness, forgot that the mermaid had told him to bring the child back to her.

One day, the child was perched on the stern of the fisherman's caique and the mermaid leapt up and seized him and took him to her den. The poor man lost his child and was left bereft.

The mermaid kept the boy until he was seventeen years of age. When he reached seventeen she brought him up to the edge of the beachfront and gave him a fish scale.

'Off with you,' she said. 'Now you can go wherever you will.'

So he set off straight back home.

When his mother saw him, and his father too, they were astonished.

But there came a day when he felt a bit constricted and hemmed in.

'Let me take off,' he said, 'and explore the orchards and the bowers.'

On and on he went and he came to a gorge. There he saw some carrion surrounded by a hog, a kite and many, many ants in wing. The animals were all fighting. When they saw him: 'How propitious it is you are here, good lad, at this very moment,' they said, 'so you can divide and share this carrion among us, because we're that close to killing one another.'

'What do I know of this business, that I should share this carrion amongst you?'

'Just get on with it and have it done: whichever way you do it, we'll abide by your ruling, such as it may be.'

So he divided up the carrion and gave the bones to the hog, and the flesh to the kite, and the belly and all the entrails to the ants.

'So now,' they said to him, 'what do we give you to thank you for the great kindness you have done us?'

The hog gave him one of its bristles and the kite gave him one of its feathers.

'Here, from me you take this wee wing,' said the ant.

'To do what with?' he says. 'What possible good could I expect from you?'

'Now,' said the ant, 'you take it, and it might be that I can do you some good at some point after all. You just see—I who you count for nothing, I will get you your dame.'

So then the lad took the wing from the ant.

'Whenever you have need of us,' they said to him, 'singe these just a little, and we will hurry to you.'

'Fine,' said he to them.

He took their offerings, hid them inside his shirt and went back to the village.

His father tells him then, 'My son, I've grown old and we need somebody to look after us. Get married for you've become a man now.'

But he didn't fancy any of the girls there.

After some while, a town crier proclaimed, 'Anyone who wishes to marry the king's daughter must resolve three matters and if he is successful he can have her. If not, the king will have his head.'

Thousands of people had gone but nobody could resolve the matters and take the daughter as wife.

On hearing the town crier, the fisherman's child said 'I shall go.'

His father wailed and expostulated, along with his mother.

'Come to your senses, child. We haven't seen our fill of you and you mean to have us lose you?'

'I shall go,' he said. 'There's no other way about it. Grant me your blessing, Father, and I shall go.'

He was given his father's blessing, along with his mother's, and then he set forth upon the way he had to go.

After several days he came to the princess, the king's daughter. You could hardly look upon her for how beautiful she was.

She held a looking glass and said, 'Hide yourself wherever you choose. I shall find the place in which you were hiding. If I find it by nine o'clock tomorrow, well and good; otherwise you can take me as your wife.'

'Alright,' said he to her, in agreement.

They signed a pact to seal it.

Then he goes to the sea, burns a bit of the fish scale, and lo, the mermaid turned up.

'What do you want?' she asked him.

'I want you to hide me,' he said, 'so I can't be seen, not at all, until nine o'clock.'

So she grabs him and takes him to her den and hides him there, putting all the fishes before him, as a mountain, so he could not be seen, not one bit.

Come morning, the princess arose, washed and at last took up the looking glass and she looked. She looked at the mountains and didn't find him, looked all over the earth's surface and couldn't find him, looks at the stars and nothing seemed to be there. She looks at the sea and just then sees fishes, lots of them, all gathered together.

'That's where he will be hiding,' she told herself. She keeps her eye right there. She became dizzy looking. 'I shall not move from here until evening,' she said.

When it was getting on to evening the fishes went to their lairs. She did not take her eye away and saw him lying inside the mermaid's den.

'So I've caught you out,' she said. 'You almost got away.'

And she went to sleep, all at ease.

In the morning he went to the princess.

'Hey,' she said to him, 'where were you hidden?'

'You be the one to find that out; I'm sure I don't know.'

'You were,' she said to him, 'in the briny sea, and a mermaid kept you in her den.'

He was flabbergasted that she'd found out.

'Fair enough,' he said to her. 'I'll hide again tomorrow and you find me if you can.'

The following day he singed the kite's feather. The bird flew directly to him.

'What do you want?' he said.

'I want you to hide me so that I can't be seen at all.'

Eagles gathered, they grabbed him and, just like that, they brought him to Africa, hid him atop a mountain and all of them gathered before him and became like a fortress.

In the morning the princess arose, washed and then took the looking glass and began looking.

'Well, well, well, let's see,' she said. 'Yesterday you really had me flummoxed; let's see how we'll manage today.'

She looked ahead of her at the sea, looked here and looked there—nothing. She couldn't see a thing, no sign at all. She looked at the sky—nothing; amongst the stars—not a thing. She looked at the mountains and, far, far away, she saw a multitude of eagles just sitting there.

'That's where he'll be,' she thought to herself. And she kept her eye glued right there.

As it was getting towards dusk the eagles started to fly away, one by one. And she saw a bit of his tarboosh, a streak of red.

'Eh! Now,' she said, 'you're not getting away anymore. I'll cut you to bits, to little pieces, because you've been very, very tiresome.'

And then she went to bed and fell asleep.

In the morning he went to the princess.

'Where were you hidden?' she said. 'You really had me exhausted, but do you know what I'll do to you?'

'You find it,' he said, 'the place where I was.'

'You were in Africa,' she said, 'and eagles kept you in their eyrie.'

'Fine,' he said. 'Let me hide one more time, and if you can find me, chop off my head.'

'Alright,' she said. 'You hide, but tomorrow I'll have mincemeat made of you.'

But it was only with her lips that she said this to him, because she had started feeling a certain fondness for him.

'What sort of a man is this,' she said, 'that can have truck with the fishes and the birds?'

The following day he singed the hog's bristle and the hog turned up.

'What do you want?' it said to him.

'I want you to hide me so that I can't be seen at all.'

He gathered all the other hogs and they dug a hole for hours and put him in there and all the hogs sat on top and made it so he couldn't be seen at all.

In the morning the princess arose, took the looking glass and sat and looked. She looked at the mountains—he couldn't be seen; she looked at the stars—nothing there; she looked into the briny sea—she couldn't find him there.

'So now, where shall I find him?' she said.

But just as she was about to give up, she saw a number of hogs at a certain spot, all piled up on one another. She looked closer and saw the hogs spreading out, for it was nearing evening and they wanted to go back to their pens. So she kept on looking until she spied his tarboosh showing a bit of red.

'So there you are,' she said. 'That's where you've been, and who would have thought it?'

She retired to her room then and went to sleep.

In the morning the lad came to the princess all gladness, because he thought she wouldn't know where he'd been.

'Where have you been?' she asked him.

'You find that out, and you tell me,' he said to her.

'You were inside a pit,' she said, 'and the hogs had you all covered up.'

'Alright,' he said. 'Let me hide this one last time, and if you can find me my head is yours. You deserve it.'

'Alright,' she said.

So he goes and singes the ant's wing and the ant came to him.

'What do you want?' he said.

'I want you to hide me,' he said.

'Put this wing in your mouth, but mind you don't go and swallow it. When you've put it in your mouth you'll become an ant yourself. Then walk up the wall and hide just behind her.'

He put the wing in his mouth and he became an ant. So he walked up the wall and stayed there just behind her.

She took up her looking glass and sat there looking. She looked here, she looked there, but he was nowhere to be seen. She looked at the sea—nothing, no sign of him; she looked at the stars—nothing; she looked at the mountains—nothing again. From morning till evening she sat and didn't budge. She was at her wits' end.

'Now, where might he be hiding?' she muttered to herself.

Up until the hour when the sun was to dip and disappear she kept peering into her looking glass. So vexed was she that she threw down her mirror and it shattered into a million shards.

'Where are you,' she said, 'that I may take you for my husband?'

He took the wing from his mouth and he was a lad again, and he hugged her in his arms.

'Here I am,' he said to her.

He took her as his wife, and so he delivered all the people who had been getting themselves killed for her sake.

The Golden-Green Eagle

Once upon a time there was an old man and he had three daughters. He was terribly poor and didn't know how to provide for his girls. So he would go and gather green herbs and sell them in town.

Well, one day, as he was gathering his greens and herbs, he happened on a huge charlock and he went over directly to uproot it. He pulled at it but it wouldn't come loose, and he had to try with all his might to yank it out of the soil.

But as he was pulling at it, there sprang a Moor from the soil, suddenly, who said to him, roughly, 'Hey, old man, what do you mean by yanking at my hair so?'

The old man stood up, beheld the Moor and was affrighted. When he came to his senses, he said, 'No, no, my Ali, I'm not yanking at your hair! I found a charlock and was trying to cut it.'

'This here charlock is my hair,' said the Moor to him. 'What do you mean to do with the greens you are gathering?'

'I have three girls,' the old man told him, 'and I provide for them with these greens that I sell.'

Then Ali gave him a handful of florins and said, 'Bring me one of your daughters and I'll make you a rich man.'

The old man was much mystified but said nothing. He went to town, bought some goods with the Moor's florins and arrived home late in the evening.

On seeing in his hands all that he had bought, his girls jumped up and down for joy and asked him how he had got hold of the money for all those things. And the old man said to them that first they should eat a proper meal and then he would explain.

After they had eaten, the old man began telling them how he had seen the Moor, how the Moor had berated him for pulling at his hair and what he'd asked for. He first asked the eldest whether she wanted to become the Moor's wife. But she burst into tears, as did the middle one. However, the third, the youngest, said, 'I shall go so you may all be delivered.'

So the following day the old man and his youngest daughter started out. And she took leave of her sisters all in tears, for she thought she would never see them again.

When they arrived at the spot where the charlock was sprouting, the old man pulled at it and then a voice was heard: 'Who is it?'

The old man responded, 'Ali, it is I and I've brought you my daughter.'

Then there was a mighty thunderclap and a great quake, and the earth below them split and forty steps were revealed.

Father and daughter started descending the stairs.

The moment they arrived at the bottom Ali appeared and said to them, 'Welcome! Fear not my girl. You'll have a wonderful time here.'

He gave the old man a bag of florins and he left. Before he went, his daughter asked him to send her sisters once in a while so that they could see one another.

The girl enjoyed herself there but every evening the Moor would give her a draught and she would drink it, and directly a deep sleep would overcome her, and she didn't see what took place then.

One day her sisters came and asked her how she was faring.

'I'm doing fine,' she said, 'but I don't know who my husband is, because every night they give me a draught to drink, and when I drink it I am overcome and I fall into a deep sleep.'

Then her sisters said to her, 'When they give you this potion, drink it not, but let it pour down your bosom into a sponge so you don't fall asleep.' And so it happened. That night she let the draught pour into the sponge and pretended to fall asleep.

Around midnight she saw a golden-green eagle come into the room, remove his wings, turn into a handsome lad and lie down beside her, having hung his keys below his chin.

When he had fallen asleep the lass stealthily removed the keys and unlocked the rooms one by one in sequence. There, inside them, she saw some women doing laundry, some women ironing and some women sewing, and she asked them why they were doing all that work. And they said to her, 'Because he'll be getting married, the golden-green eagle will.'

Then, once she had locked up again, full of joy, she went to put the keys back in their place, but just then the golden-green eagle woke up and he called the Moor, furiously, and said, 'Ali, Ali, the woman you brought me is not for me.' And Ali took her and threw her out into the night.

Upon finding herself alone in the wilderness, Marió (that was the poor girl's name) started to weep.

But the golden-green eagle must have taken pity on her, for he went close to her and told her, 'Come, let me kiss you and instruct you.' And he gave her a little cup of honey and a fig and said to her, 'You will go and find my mother sitting at her balcony and spinning, and you will pass the yarn through the honey and she'll taste its sweetness and will tell you, "Whoever has sweetened me, let them be sweetened," and you will say "It is I". And she will tell you to go up to her and you will tell her, "If I am to come up to you, swear to me upon the golden-green eagle that you won't eat me." '

So Marió picked herself up, wiped away her tears and walked up the road and walked down the road and found herself at a place where she saw an ogress sitting at a balcony and spinning silk. Then she ran, hid beneath the balcony and, into the honey the golden-green eagle had given her, she dipped the yarn the old ogress let fall. She, on passing it through her mouth, tasted the sweetness and said, 'Who sweetened me, may they be sweetened.'

Then the lass stepped out of her hiding place and said to her, 'It is I.'

'Come on up to me; I won't eat you,' said the ogress to her.

'First you must vow to me that you will not eat me,' said Marió.

So the ogress started swearing a vow, 'By my vineyards, by my fields, by my houses I won't eat you.'

'No,' said Marió to her, 'you swear to me by the golden-green eagle, and then I'll come up.'

Once the ogress had vowed 'by the golden-green eagle I shall not eat you' she went up.

The following day the ogress went out to hunt and told her, 'In the evening, when I return I want to find the swept unswept. If you fail to do that, I shall eat you.'

Then Marió started to weep—how to get the swept unswept?

Around midday the golden-green eagle arrived and asked her, 'What is the matter, Marió? Why you are crying?'

'What could be the matter, here where you've bade me come? Your mother told me to get the swept unswept and if I fail to get it done, as she wants, she'll eat me.'

'Come, let me kiss you and tutor you. You will sweep the entire house good and proper and then you'll gather all the sweepings in the middle and you'll give them a push this way once and a push that way once, and the swept will get unswept. And when she asks you who taught you, you tell her, "I knew how and so I did so".'

In the evening the ogress returned, looked at the house and found the swept unswept and said to her:

'Either you know sorcery and spells
or you are a warlock's daughter
or this is the teaching of the golden-green eagle.'
'Neither do I know sorcery or spells
nor a warlock's daughter am I
nor is this the teaching of the golden-green eagle.
I knew how and so I did so.'

The next day the ogress left her the birds she'd brought back from hunting and told her, 'You get these cooked uncooked. If you fail to do that, I shall eat you.'

That got Marió crying once more. How to get the cooked uncooked?

Around midday the golden-green eagle arrived again, saw her weeping and said to her, 'Whatever's the matter, Marió my sweet? Why are you crying?'

'What could be the matter, here where you bade me come? Your mother told me to get the cooked uncooked and if I fail to get it done as she wants, she'll eat me.'

'Come, let me kiss you and instruct you. You will take the birds and pluck and clean them and then you'll take half and cook them and when they are done you will add the other half. And when she asks you who taught you to do this, you tell her, "I knew how and so I did so".'

And that's exactly what Marió did.

In the evening the ogress returned, saw the cooked uncooked and said to her:

'Either you know sorcery and spells
or you are a warlock's daughter
or this is the teaching of the golden-green eagle.'
'Neither do I know sorcery or spells,
nor a warlock's daughter am I,
nor is this the teaching of the golden-green eagle.
I knew how and so I did so.'

The following day the ogress gave her forty pairs of pillows to wash, to iron and to stuff with down.

Marió started weeping again, and the golden-eagle came by and said to her, 'What is the matter Marió? Why are you crying?'

'What could be the matter, here where you bade me come? Your mother told me to get forty pairs of pillows ready without giving me anything, neither water, nor soap, nor any down to stuff them with.'

'Come, let me kiss you and instruct you. You'll go down this road and you will reach a spring. There you will wash the forty pairs of pillows, dry them and then cry out loud, "Birds of the plain and of Roumeli, come preen your plumage for the golden-green eagle is to be married". The birds will come then and will preen their plumage, and you will gather the down and stuff the pillows.'

And so she did exactly so. She went to the spring, washed the forty pairs of pillows, dried them and called the birds of the plain and of Roumeli and they preened their plumage, and she gathered the down and so stuffed the pillows.

That evening, when the ogress came back, she found all in readiness and she said to her:

'Either you know sorcery and spells
or you are a warlock's daughter
or this is the teaching of the golden-green eagle.'

'Neither do I know sorcery or spells,
nor a warlock's daughter am I,
nor is this the teaching of the golden-green eagle.
I knew how and so I did so.'

The following day she says to her, 'You will go to my sister to fetch me the instruments, the drums, for the golden-green eagle is to be married. If you fail to fetch them I shall eat you.'

Once again Marió began to weep. The golden-green eagle came by and instructed her. 'You'll take this path,' he said to her, 'and once you've progressed far, as far is far, you'll find a maggoty spring. You'll stoop and you'll drink the water and you'll say, "Such wonderful fresh water! Never in my life have I drunk such lovely water". Then you'll walk some more, as more is more and you'll find a maggoty apple tree. You'll pick an apple and you'll eat it and you'll say, "Such a wonderful apple! Never in my life have I eaten such a lovely apple". Then you'll walk still further and you'll find masses of thorns, so thick you won't be able to pass through. Then you'll say, "Roses, oh, you gorgeous blooms, stand aside that I may pass", and they will withdraw their thorns so that you may pass. And then, finally, you will reach a house, and outside it you'll find a donkey gnawing at some bones and a dog grazing on some hay. You will take the hay and put it before the donkey and you will take the bones and put them before the dog. Then you'll find the stairs that haven't been swept for ages and ages and you'll sweep them with your apron and you'll mount them. Once you get to the door, you will knock and my aunt, the lamia, the big old ogress, will come out and ask you, "What do you want?".

'"Your sister has sent me", you will tell her, "so that you give me the instruments, the drums, for the golden-green eagle is to be married". She will go back inside then, not in order to bring them for you but to file her teeth. You will seize the instruments and the drums hanging behind the door and leave at once. As she sees you leaving with the instruments, the drums, she will start screaming furiously, "Stairs, throw her down". They will tell her, "How can we throw her down when you'd left us unswept for years and years, and she swept us?". "Dog eat her; ass kill her!" They will speak thus to her: "How can we kill her, when she gave us our proper food while you had it switched around all these years!" Then she will scream, "Thorns, pour your poison and poison her". "How can we possibly poison her, the one who said to us, for the very first time: 'Roses, oh you gorgeous blooms', when you have been berating us all these years!". "Maggoty apple tree, throw your apples at her and kill her!". "How could I kill her when she ate one of my apples and said how wonderful it was, whereas you've never ever eaten even one!". "Maggoty spring, pour out your water and drown her!" "How can I drown her when she drank of my water and said it was lovely, and you've never drunk even a single sip!" And thus you will make your way and bring the instruments, the drums, to my mother.'

That's what he said, and then he left. And Marió set forth, and walked and walked and found the maggoty spring first, bent down, drank and said, 'Such wonderful water!' Then she found the maggoty apple tree and picked a few apples and ate and said, 'Such a wonderful apple!' and did everything as instructed by the golden-green eagle and brought all the instruments and drums.

When the ogress saw that she'd brought the instruments, the drums, she gnashed her teeth and said to her:

'Either you know sorcery and spells
or you are a warlock's daughter
or this is the teaching of the golden-green eagle.'
'Neither do I know sorcery or spells,
nor a warlock's daughter am I,
nor is this the teaching of the golden-green eagle.
I knew how and so I brought them,' said Marió.

The following day was to be the wedding of the golden-green eagle with an ogress maiden. Huge preparations. The ogress maiden arrived, and the wedding was held.

That very evening, before they lay down to sleep, the ogress mother placed ten candles on Marió's fingers, one on each, and lit them so they would illuminate the bridal chamber. She told her that if the candles were to drip on her fingers she should not cry out, for if she heard just the slightest sound coming from her, ah!, she would arise and eat her.

Marió stood there and brightened the room with the candles on her fingers as the ogress had demanded and was careful no cry escaped her lips. But after some considerable while, when the candles started dripping and she bit her lips to stifle her pain, the golden-green eagle nudged the ogress maiden. 'Get up,' he said, 'and give her a break, the poor thing, and then you can come back to bed.'

So she got up and took the candles, but the moment one of them dripped on her fingers for the first time she let out a cry of pain for having been scalded. Directly the ogress rushed into the room and ate the one that held the candles, for she thought it was Marió. Her son pretended to be distressed and shed a few tears saying, 'Woe is me, my mother. You've eaten my bride.' And promptly the ogress exploded for her spite. So the golden-green eagle took Marió for his wife and they had a lovely time of it and we had a lovelier one still.

The Owl and the Partridge

One day all the birds gathered together and agreed to send their offspring to school to learn their letters. They found a master and appointed him. The school opened and they took their fledglings there and enrolled them as pupils.

A few days later several fledglings turned up in class without having done their homework. The master kept them in at midday, letting them go hungry.

Among the fledglings that were punished was the owl's child.

The owl, seeing that school was done for the afternoon, and that her baby had not been let out, took some bread with her and went to the schoolhouse to bring it to her child.

On her way there she bumped into the partridge. Her baby had also been kept fasting and she was going to bring it some bread too.

Said the partridge to the owl, 'My good neighbour, long may you enjoy your eyesight, I have such a lot to get done and I'm practically rushed off my feet. Would you please be so kind as to take my baby's food with you to give to it?'

'That I would, good neighbour, willingly,' said the owl. 'It's just that I don't know which one is your baby.'

'Oh,' said the partridge, 'that's the easiest thing for you to ken. Mine is the most outstandingly good-looking baby in the school!'

The owl went to the school. She entreated the master and he agreed to have the bread given to her baby. Then she asked the master to let her have a look at all the other fledglings. She looked them over carefully but couldn't find the partridge's child.

She arrived back home and went to seek out the partridge. She gave her back the bread, saying, 'What a to-do. What was I to do? I spent a whole hour looking and I couldn't find your baby, because in the whole school there was no more good-looking baby than my own!'

Crab and Snake

Once upon a time a snake went down to the beach and happened to meet a crab and said to him, 'Poor old crab, I want to have one of you marine creatures as an in-law, so that I can come down here once in a while and eat a bite of seafood and then, if he likes, he can visit me in my lair and help himself to a bite or two of succulent greens. Hey, what do you say? Shall we become in-laws?'

And the crab, upon thinking it over, agreed. 'Yes, let's do it,' he said.

They joined their hands in a handshake in token of their agreement and directly sat down to eat. The crab brought him a variety of seafood and shrimps and sea greens.

When they had finished eating the snake was in great good cheer and wouldn't stop drinking toasts. 'Here's to you, my goodly crab-in-law' and 'here's to you, my fine crab-in-law', he would say, hugging the poor crab.

The crab-in-law, who happened to be of a somewhat shy disposition, would say to him, 'That's quite a grip you've got there, snake-in-law.'

'But I'm so terribly fond of you, crab-in-law,' said the snake to him.

Then again, after a little while: 'Here's to you, my crab-in-law.' And he kept squeezing him.

'You do squeeze tight, my snake-in-law, and I think I'll burst.'

And the snake, who knew what he was about: 'I can't help it, crab-in-law. I'm so very, very fond of you.'

'I'm fond of you too, snake-in-law,' the crab said back, but he could tell that something was amiss: the snake kept squeezing him tighter as time went by and would not relax its grip at all.

And again, a moment or two later he squeezed the crab, so that the crab, in desperation, turned round and gripped the snake's neck in its claws and that was when the snake let go and stretched in the crab's lair for as long as its length.

Then the crab said to him, 'There, it's better like this! Keep straight, snake-in-law, not in coils looking to smother me!'

Boughs of Gold

Once upon a time there was a baker and she had a child. After she was left a widow, poor as a church mouse, she kept toiling at her bakery. She would trek to the hills, gather twigs and carry them to the village, fire the oven, bake this woman's bread, that woman's daily fare, be paid a little bit of money, and with that make do for herself and for her child.

One day she got herself ready to go to the hills. The child began bawling: 'I want to go too! I want to go too!' His mother didn't want to take him along. She said to him, 'I'm not going to take you along! Don't you think of coming with me for there is no water. You'll get thirsty and there'll be nothing to drink!'

'No,' said the child, 'I won't get thirsty, but even if I do I shan't ask for water. I'll let you do your work and I shall drink water only when we return to the village! Take me along and you'll see!'

So she took the child along with her. When they reached the hills the child ran, played, got tired and sat down to eat a couple of olives and some bread his mother gave him.

Once he ate he became thirsty but said nothing to his mother. He stood up and started looking around to see whether there was anywhere he could find a little water. On the opposite side of the slope, a little further down, he saw a castle. Its gate was open, there was a lush grove inside it, and between the trees and the flowers a stream was flowing through.

Joyously, he went to his mother and said to her, 'There, Mother, I've found me some water in that castle there. I shall go and have a drink!'

His mother let out a howl. She entreated him not to go for the castle was enchanted. Everybody that went inside to drink water found the gate shutting behind them and disappeared: nobody ever came back. She begged the child, told him they should make their return, go back to the village.

'Let me tie up these faggots, make bundles of the sticks,' she said to him. 'We'll take them up on our shoulders and we'll leave directly! My child, don't go into the castle, for I will lose you if you do!'

The child pretended he wasn't going to go. The mother bent to tie the twigs into bundles and the child gave her the slip, went to the castle and drank of the water. When his thirst was slaked he made for the exit, but the gate had shut. He cried and called for his mother. She rushed to the castle, banged on the gate and begged with many an entreaty, but all to no avail! The mother kept circling the castle, going round and round, calling after her child.

When the child saw that the gate wouldn't open, he thought he'd better head further off, just in case there was another gate to let himself out. He went in a different direction from his mother; she lost sight of him! The mother stayed on late, until dusk. When she realized her child had disappeared, she left and went back to the village, her heart filled with grief.

Let us leave the mother to her woe, as she wept at losing her child, and at being left all on her own like a lone reed in the middle of a field, and let us see what happened to the child. He went around trying to find a place to let himself out. Night fell, he felt tired, his strength had left him what with walking and what with crying, and so he lay down under a tree, turned on his side and fell asleep.

At dawn a monster came out, an ogre, from inside the castle. He saw the child and went up close. The ogre looked him over, felt his arms, his body and said, 'It's a bit on the scrawny side. I need to fatten it before I can eat it!' It gave the child a nudge, and said to him, 'Get up. Let's go inside.'

Yannaki was irate. 'Whatever are you nudging me and shoving me for? What should I be getting up for? I'm still feeling sleepy. Let me lie down a while longer!'

'Get up at once. What are you playing at, as if you were something special!' said the ogre.

The child didn't bat an eyelid. He sat up under the tree, his back resting against the trunk.

'I'm not going anywhere,' he said. 'I'm fine and comfy here. Come and get me if you dare!'

The ogre lunged at the child, grabbing hold of him and planting him up to the ankles in the soil. Yannaki grabbed hold of the ogre, gave him a mighty blow and planted him in the earth up to the knees.

Said the ogre, 'That's it! You've defeated me! I shall have to leave. Everything in here is yours now. Take these keys; there are forty of them. You may open thirty-nine of the cabinets that you'll find in the castle. Whatever you find in there is yours. Mind though that you don't open the last one for that will mean your doom. Everybody that opened it was removed to the place from which there is no coming back, and they were never ever seen again! In the first cabinet you shall find the brogues that, when worn, make you noiseless; the cap that, when worn, makes you vanish; and the unbeatable sword, which, when drawn, defeats and kills everybody. Put them on and go then to the paddock. There you will find the horse that speaks like a human. When he sees you girded with the sword he'll know you for his master and he'll take you wherever you please.'

And having said all this the ogre vanished. Yannaki was left thunderstruck. He could not make head or tail of all the ogre had told him. He took up the keys and then set himself to thinking. It occurred to him all this might be a dream. Then he said to himself, 'Let me go and open up those cabinets and see what I find there.'

He opened up one of them, then another. He found the sword, the cap, the brogues. He found sweetmeats, fruit, food. He found clothes made from cloth of gold, he found florins and jewels and all sorts of wondrous things. He also found four golden apples that the ogre had told him represented his destiny: as long as he was well the apples would be luscious and red and their leaves green and fresh; were he to fall ill or be in jeopardy they would wither and shed their leaves. He took those along with him too.

He opened all thirty-nine cabinets and reached the last one. He held the key and thought, 'Shall I open it? Shall I not?' He was of two minds. Finally he said, 'Why not open it? See how many things I've found in the other thirty-nine! Just think what treasures there'll be in this one here! Didn't the ogre tell me that I should have everything and that this one was the only one I oughtn't to touch! I will open it to see what's inside it!'

He put the key in the lock and opened it! The moment it was opened the place was struck with ineffable brilliance! Shut in there was a girl, the fairest in the world, and she was gazing at him! He made as if to touch her, but she stretched out her arms and pushed him away.

'Don't you touch me. You are not yet worthy to be mine. I shall leave and I will go to the boughs of gold. If you prove worthy and come and find them where they are, then I will become yours!' And directly she turned into a will-o'-the-wisp, a plume of smoke, and vanished from before his very eyes.

On losing her Yannaki almost lost his mind.

Such loveliness to behold and that he should have lost her! 'I shall find the boughs of gold even if I have to journey the world over!' he said. 'I'm not letting go of her.' He girded himself with the sword, put on the brogues, grabbed the cap and went down to the paddock. He found the horse, bid it good morning and, to get into its favour, treated it to some of the sweetmeats he had found in the cabinets. He said, 'My good steed, I would like you to take me to find the boughs of gold! I know that you know everything; I know it well.'

'I shall take you wherever you wish,' said the horse to him. 'I know all of the wide world, but I know of no boughs of gold. Abandon this notion; it doesn't bode well for you. We shan't be able to find them.'

Yannaki, though, was fixed on his notion, and he kept saying, 'I want us to go; I need us to go, my dearest steed, and find the boughs of gold. Please, I beg of you, please take me there!'

Then the steed said, 'Very well then. If that be your wish, let us go, and may God help us.'

On and on and on they went, and still they kept going. The steed was fond of Yannaki and was well pleased to have a human for master rather than the ogre. He talked to Yannaki, and counselled him on the right thing to do and how to comport himself.

There came a dawn and they were at a certain place, and at sunrise they saw a rider, far-off, astride a white horse and he was approaching. Said the steed, 'You see that rider there? He is the son of the sun. When he draws closer and comes near you, give him a clout and then bid him good morning.'

Yannaki found this odd but didn't argue, for he knew that the steed always spoke rightly.

As the rider came up, Yannaki dealt him a resounding wallop and then said, 'Good morning, brother!'

'Well met, my good brother! Where are you off to?' the sun's son replied.

'I'm off to find the boughs of gold and I know not where they might be,' said Yannaki.

'I shall go along with you, brother,' said the sun's son. 'The trouble is that I don't know where they may be either.'

So henceforth they were as brothers. The son of the sun followed Yannaki. He regarded him as his captain. With the blow he'd given him he had established himself as the chief. They rode all day long.

On and on and on they went, and still they kept going. As dusk was falling, at sundown, they saw a rider on a silver horse and he was heading toward them. Said the steed once again to Yannaki, 'See that lad there? That is the moon's son. Now, you give him a clout too, otherwise he won't acknowledge you as leader and he'll be challenging you to fight it out to see who beats the other.'

Yannaki dealt him a mighty wallop and said, 'Good evening, brother!'

He joined their company so now there were three of them.

When they reached the coast they found another rider. He was the sea's son. The steed gave Yannaki the same advice again. He whacked the rider and made him his brother. And he went along with them.

So now there were four and Yannaki was their leader.

They roamed from one place to another, seeking to find the boughs of gold. But no matter where they went, no matter who they asked, nobody had anything useful to tell them.

Time was passing and Yannaki was distressed at having the three lads roaming along with him and suffering all sorts of trials and hardship.

One day they reached a township and heard the town crier proclaiming, 'Whoever crosses this stream with a horse—jumps across to the other bank and comes back—shall have the princess as his wife.'

On hearing that Yannaki said, 'It'd be good to see to the future of one of my brothers. He could marry the princess and stay on here and be king. He has spent many years toiling with me.'

He went to his horse, patted it, sweet-talked it and asked, 'My beloved steed, what do you say? Can you jump over the stream that we may be given the princess as bride for my brother?'

Said the horse, 'It isn't easy, but yes, I shall jump over the stream.'

Yannaki presented himself to the king and said, 'I shall jump and if I win, my brother, the son of the sun, is to have the princess.'

The king agreed.

Yannaki gave a leap with his horse and there he was across on the opposite bank. He gave one more leap and there he was, back to where he'd started from! Huzzas, celebrations, applause.

They all stayed on, the betrothal took place and then the wedding. It was a time of joyous festival.

A month passed and Yannaki said, 'Brother, I'll be on my way now. I'm leaving you this apple. So long as it keeps fresh and hale, it means I'm fine. If you see it wrinkling and its leaves turning yellow it means some evil has befallen me. If in truth you love me, take the road across from the sun, due east, and go in search of me, until you find me alive or dead.'

The three of them set out. On and on and on they went, and they asked after the boughs of gold, but didn't find them. Quite some time passed and again they arrived at a township and heard a town crier proclaiming, 'Anybody who can spend the whole night sleepless, close to the princess, and see where she goes and what she does each evening when she is off to bed will have her for his wife.'

The princess was under an enchantment and she did not wish to marry. She had been put under a spell by an ogre and she had no eyes for any man in the world. Every night he went to her and took her away, and nobody knew where they went or what they did all night long. Her father wanted to marry her off, but she would have none of it. They had a wager, she and the king, that she would take for husband whoever managed to follow her and see where she went every night. Anybody who fell asleep though, and couldn't stay awake, would have to lose his head.

Up to the time when Yannaki arrived thirty-nine princes had presented themselves and the princess had erected a grisly cairn made of their heads. If she had one more head chopped, that would make forty, and the cairn would be done, and the king had given her his word that he wouldn't bother her any longer, and would never bring up the topic of marriage again.

On hearing the herald, Yannaki said, 'It would be good if I were to have my brother, the son of the moon, marry this princess.'

So Yannaki went to the king and said he wanted to stay close to the princess and remain awake, and if he managed to find where the princess went, then his brother, the son of the moon, should marry her.

The king, feeling very sorry for Yannaki, urged him not to go. It would be a shame for such a handsome, good-natured lad as this to lose his life. Yannaki, however, would have none of it. So they agreed he should go that evening and, if victorious, his brother should have the princess.

Yannaki got ready, went to his horse and asked it how he should go about things so as to remain wakeful. The horse warned him that he should be extra careful not to drink of the coffee they would offer him, but to feign drinking it and pour it away. He must then seem as if he'd gone to sleep, and when the princess got up to go he should follow behind her and see to it that he obtain some sign in witness of where he'd been so as to be able to prove the truth of his words.

'Lest she hear you as you go with her put on your brogues, which cannot be heard as you walk, and your cap, which renders you invisible.'

'Thank you, my good old steed,' said Yannaki. He patted him, gave him sweetmeats, hugged him and left.

Come evening, Yannaki went to the princess's room and she offered him a cup of coffee. Yannaki poured it down his neck into his shirt, where he had hidden a sponge to catch the liquid. After some time had passed he pretended to be yawning and that he could hardly stay awake. He lay down and made it seem as if he were snoring.

'Ah, there he goes just like all the others!' said the princess.

At midnight he heard a rumble and saw the fireplace split in two. Out of it came a ferocious ogre, a veritable hulk, who said, 'Good evening, my sweet lovey dove, my dearest!'

'Good evening, my love,' said she to him. 'What do you say? Is it time?'

They embraced and passed through the cleft in the fireplace. Yannaki stood up, put on his cap, put on his brogues and went along. They got into a coach and Yannaki followed right behind them.

They arrived at a fine bower, stepped down from the coach and there was a table set and waiting for them. They sat down to eat. Yannaki was at the princess's side. The ogre served her with food and then more food... and Yannaki ate from her plate. Before you could turn around, the plate had emptied!

Said the ogre, 'What an appetite you have this evening, my beloved! I can hardly keep up with you as I serve you this repast.'

'It is for joy,' said the princess. 'Tonight my father's deadline expires. With the duffer that's sleeping in my room I'll have my forty heads. My cairn will be done and my father has given me his word he will never ever talk to me again about getting married. So then you can come to the palace every night and be with me. Nobody shall interfere.'

The ogre said, 'I shall give you this egg and if you ever want me to come to you during the day, at any hour, just crack it and I will appear at once.'

The princess took the egg, put it in her pocket and said, 'Whatever you want I shall do for your sake. I'd even walk into a blazing fire were you to ask me to!'

In the middle of their blandishments and their dilly-dallying Yannaki bent over, removed the egg from her pocket and thrust it inside his shirt. They had no inkling.

Close to daybreak they got up and, once again, set off in the coach. They returned to the palace and entered her room through the fireplace.

Yannaki passed to the front, entering before they did, lying down, removing the cap and pretending to be deep in sleep.

The princess went to her bed, lay down and fell asleep, as did Yannaki until the sun was up.

Then the king arrived to unlock. He swung the door open and found himself before his daughter, who had just awakened.

'Come, Father,' she said, 'take this one away too. Off to the block with him to have his head chopped off so I can have it to complete my cairn. I've beaten you at our wager!'

Sorrowfully the king nudged Yannaki awake. Yannaki opened his eyes, saw the king and the soldiers all about him.

He sat up and said, 'Forgive me, Your Majesty, I spent all night traipsing about, trailing after your daughter and I am dead tired, so I fell asleep!'

'What's all this you're talking about?' said the princess. 'You dropped off sound asleep and you didn't wake up at all in the night! Was all of this in your dreams as you lay there asleep?'

So then Yannaki began recounting to the king how the hearth was cleft at the corner, about the ogre, everything. The princess denied it all... Yannaki spoke of the bower, of the table. The princess nearly had a fit, so mortified was she. How could Yannaki have seen all that and she hadn't spied him at it? She kept on denying everything.

'And to prove to you that all this is true,' said Yannaki, 'here is this egg, my king. Crack it and you'll see. The ogre will come here and you shall see him with your own eyes, and give me credence.'

On hearing about the egg, the princess felt for it in her pocket: it was nowhere to be found! She collapsed in a swoon.

The king took the egg, cracked it and at once there appeared the monster of an ogre! The moment they beheld him everyone's blood curdled. In his concern for her, seeing she had fainted, he rushed to her side and sought to hold her in his arms. Yannaki saw his chance, pulled out his sword and dealt him a deft blow that cut his head clean off.

The princess came to. She opened her eyes and fell into her father's embrace, released at last from the enchantment! Rejoicing, laughter all around. A few days later they held her nuptials to the son of the moon. Singing, dancing, music, feasting…

A month or so must have gone by. Yannaki got himself ready, along with the son of the sea, girded his sword, took hold of his horse and all his belongings, bid the king goodbye and took leave of his brother and his wife, the princess. He left an apple with him too, and explained that if it were seen to wither, he should await their other brother, the son of the sun, so they could set off together to look for him. They embraced, bid each other adieu and he was on his way.

On and on they went, just the two of them. Turning this way, turning that way, they reached a kingdom where the princess chose not to speak and the king had proclaimed, 'Whosoever can manage to make the princess speak shall have her for his wife, otherwise his life shall be forfeit!'

Yannaki asked his horse once again, 'My good old steed, how can I induce the princess to break her silence, so I can marry her to my brother that he too may find rest and leave off sharing our trials and hardship?'

'This is the most difficult undertaking of all,' said the horse. 'There is only one way for you to achieve it. Tell the king to cause a two-way mirror cabinet to be made for you, and in there you will conceal the son of the sea,

and when you find that you cannot make the princess speak, around daybreak, you will address the mirror and say, "Mirror, mirror mine, seeing the princess will say naught to me, why do *you* not speak to me and offer me consolation, this being my last night. Would you tell me a story that I may forget my grief?" And then the son of the sea can start to speak to you from within the mirror, and perhaps the princess will be impelled by curiosity and will speak as well, to find out how it is that the mirror can speak.'

Yannaki had everything done as instructed by the horse. The king caused the mirror to be wrought, the companion shut himself in and, as dark fell, they took the mirror into the princess's room. Then Yannaki entered as well. He began to speak to her, to entreat her, to tell her funny stories. The princess remained silent! You might think she was hardly even there!

As dawn was approaching, as he saw that all his words were in vain, Yannaki turned to the mirror and said, 'My good mirror, seeing that the people here are so hard-hearted and have no pity for me, as young as I am and destined to die, and they speak not one word to me, you speak to me, you, who have no soul of your own, and so keep me company!'

The son of the sea spoke up from within the mirror and said, 'And what would you have me tell you?'

'Tell me a story to while away the time until daybreak comes, when I am doomed to be put to death,' said Yannaki.

Said the mirror, 'Very gladly will I tell you one:

Once upon a time a poor man had one precious and only child. Poverty and no work at all. He grew desperate and said to his wife, "I shall take the child and bring him to the town to get apprenticed to a trade, so that he won't have to go hungry when he grows up."

He took the child, but money they had none, so they had to go on their way on foot. Along the way, at Alortho Pouri (a beach in Skyros) they felt tired, so they sat down to have something to eat and to rest for a while. The father, distraught as he was at the prospect of leaving his child in strange hands, heaved a deep sigh and said, "Alas, alas and thrice alas!"

On having said that, he saw the sea swelling up and a wave as tall as a mountain coming at him. He was frightened and ready to flee!

But before having a chance to do so, the wave broke up and out of it sprang forth a fearsome sprite, who said to him, "Why have you summoned me? What would you have of me?"

The poor father was frightened stiff and said to him, "I did not mean to address you, My Lord. I just sighed and said, 'Alas! Alas and thrice alas!' for my great misfortune and for my poverty that shall deprive me of my child, now that I go to leave him alone in strange hands until he learns himself a trade."

The sprite said, "Seeing as you have summoned me, I shall help you. I shall take your child along with me and teach him a trade. In two years' time you will come back to this same place and call me to get your child back."

He strode off, yanking the child along with him, and headed down beneath the surface of the sea, back to his palace. That's where he kept the other children he had been abducting for some while now, all turned into stone from below their waist. He set the child to serve the others, told him what he had to do and told him too that he was to take care not to touch a cabinet that stood in one corner, and particularly not to touch the books in there, for if he did a great evil would befall him.

The child, who was clever, mused, "Why not see whether I can read those books, find out what's in them and learn from them myself, and have my eyes opened?"

So he began to read. The books were magical and Alas had warned him not to touch them, fearing he would encroach on his art. But the child, being clever, did read them, learning sorceries and enchantments, not just the ones Alas knew but an additional one too. He learnt to know what another was thinking.

The two years passed and the father came back to Alortho Pouri and called out.

Alas emerged and said, "Let's go so you can see your child."

They went down to his palace and he called the child. Rejoicing, kisses, embraces.

But the child, having learnt to discern what another was thinking, realized what Alas meant to do, and said to his father, "Father, this one here doesn't mean to hand me over to you. Along with the other children he has gathered and keeps shut up in this place, he will turn me into a pony and he will test you, asking you whether you can recognize me. Know this, I'll have stepped up to the very front and I'll be the first pony. When he asks you which is your child you will know and you will be able to point to me."

So Alas joined them after a short while and said to the father, "Isn't it time you were on your way?"

Says the father, "I'll leave, but I'll take my son along too."

"If you can tell me which your child is among the other children, now that I'll show you all of them together, you can have him. I'll give him back to you!" said Alas.

He took him and brought him to a wide meadow. A little later there arrived about a hundred ponies. Said Alas, "All of them are human children, and I've put a spell on them and turned them into ponies. Which of them is yours?"

The old man went close to the ponies and looked them over one by one. He made it look as if he was searching for his son. Finally he pointed to the one at the front.

"This be my child." And indeed, that was the one!

Seeing that he recognized him, what else could Alas do? He brought them up to the surface and let them go, and so they went on their way.

Along the way, as they were heading towards their village, they saw a peasant walking ahead of them.

Said the child to his father, "Father, look: I am fairly well versed in enchantments now, so I'll turn into a pony and you can sell me to that peasant, and we can get us ten pounds, and then I'll leave him and become a human being again, and we can keep the money."

They agreed, the child turned into a pony, and the old man pulled it along by a halter.

The peasant said to him, "Friend, are you selling that pony?"

"Good you've asked. Yes, I'm selling it. Give me ten pounds and he's yours."

The peasant gave him the ten pounds, took the pony and went. Secretly, the father followed them to see what would come about.

As the peasant had him tied to the halter and was pulling him, the child started rubbing his muzzle on the man's hands and licking them.

Said the peasant to himself, "This one knows me for its master already. I will let it go free for a little."

The moment he undid the halter the pony sped away and the man was left behind. The pony turned into a child again, went to his father and said to him, "Let's go now, quick," and they sped away.

The peasant ran around, came back, looked here, looked there—no luck!

Right then Alas turned up too. He was coming after the child in an attempt to get him back. He had regretted having let him go. The moment the peasant asked him whether he'd seen a pony that looked like so, he realized it was the child and that he had learnt how to work magic.

Alas turned at once into a hawk and flew off to find the child. The child saw him coming. He turned into an eagle and fell upon Alas. Alas became a bigger bird of prey and struggled to gobble up the eagle. The child turned into two seeds and one fell into the pinafore of the princess, who was sitting in the garden, and the other fell on the ground.

Directly Alas turned into a pigeon, jumped into the princess's pinafore and pecked at the seed in her lap and gobbled it up. But before it had hopped onto the ground to eat the other one, the one that held the child, the child turned to a falcon, grabbed the pigeon in its talons, ripped it apart and tore it to shreds.

There went Alas; that was the end of him. The child was released and everybody was freed from the spells that had held them, and they lived on happily ever after!

There, did you enjoy my tale?' asked the mirror.

'Thank you, my good old mirror. It was really, really first-rate!' said Yannaki.

When the mirror had started talking the princess had quit her seat, and come up close. She gazed now on the mirror, now on Yannaki. She couldn't understand it. How could this wonder be happening? And as she gazed on Yannaki, and saw him so handsome, she started taking a liking to him and began to feel a little sorry for him, destined as he was to be put to death. And then again, it wouldn't do to let on that she had taken a shine to him! But it so happened that she could hardly hold herself back for her curiosity. She was making it look as if her eyes were on the looking glass, but it was Yannaki she kept her eyes on, mirrored in the looking glass.

When the tale was over she blurted, 'But how can it be that a mirror talks?'

Yannaki got up then, went to her, and said, 'There, I've beaten you, my princess!'

She didn't want to admit it. The moment she spoke she regretted it and clamped her mouth shut again. She just sat there in her place and wouldn't say a word.

Said Yannaki, 'I've beaten you. You spoke to me! And I have a witness too.' He went and opened the mirror and brought the son of the sea out of it. And he said, 'This is the one that beat you, who spoke from inside the mirror. This is the one that shall be your husband.'

What was the princess to do now? She had to concede. They came out of her room together and went to the king. Yannaki had them married to one another, and left the son of the sea an apple. Now he went on his way entirely on his own. His only companion was his horse. That was who he spoke to and the horse would counsel him what he ought to be doing.

On and on they rode . . . There came a morning when they reached the end of the world. Beyond the borders of the world the horse saw something glinting in the sun.

He said to Yannaki, 'I do believe that is a bough of gold. What do you say? Shall I head yonder?'

'Let's go,' said Yannaki.

They came out of this world and approached the glinting. As they approached they saw an entire arbour of boughs of gold, a tower in its middle and around it a grove of trees, all with boughs of gold. A real paradise. Outside of the door to the tower a crone was seated. Seeing Yannaki she was quite astonished.

She said to him, 'However did you get here?'

'I came to find the boughs of gold to win the fairest in the world. Do you know where she might be?'

'She's here,' said the crone. 'Wait; I'll tell her you are here.' She went in and told her, then fetched Yannaki and they went inside. Yannaki couldn't get his fill of looking at her.

Said the fairest in the world: 'Since you have proven yourself worthy by reaching here and you've succeeded in finding me, you are my husband now.'

They lived together from then on. She came to love him and for his sake she became a woman like all other women. She stopped being a will-o'-the-wisp, and she transported the orchard with the boughs of gold, along with her tower, close to the people who reside in this world of ours.

Yannaki was mad with love of her. He couldn't stay away from her for even one instant. She urged him to go out, to go hunting, to stop stifling himself all shut up indoors, to see other people now that they were back in the world again.

He explained that he couldn't stay away from her for even one single moment; he needed always to be feasting his eyes on her.

'Is that all?' said the girl. 'Wait; I'll give you a picture of me so you can carry it around with you wherever you might find yourself.'

She handed him her picture; he hid it in his shirt and went hunting. Yannaki roamed the mountainside, hunted, scrambled up slopes, climbed down, got tired, got thirsty. He found a spring, stooped to drink water and sat a while to rest. But as he stooped to drink the picture fell out of his shirt. He didn't notice. He rested for a brief moment, then rose to go. He returned to the palace and to his wife.

That evening the king's grooms drove the horses to the spring for them to drink, but they wouldn't. They shied and kept backing away. The grooms arrived back at the palace and the king wanted to know if the horses had drunk, so they told him what had happened. The king took the horses and went to the spring on his own. He stooped to have a look and see what might be wrong with the water that they wouldn't drink, and he found the picture. Having seen it, he sent out a herald with the news and the proclamation that anybody that could tell him who she was and where she might be found would be given half his kingdom.

The crone that served the fairest in the world had

gone to the market and she heard the herald and went to the king.

She said to him, 'I'll bring her to you. But I must have some troops to carry her away for she will be unwilling, so I'll need them to help me and do my bidding.'

The troops went along and the crone hid them in the tower.

The following day Yannaki rode off to go hunting. When he came back, tired out, he ate and went to lie down.

His lady was sitting close by him, embroidering, when the crone said to her, 'Come on downstairs, my lady, to do your handiwork, lest you waken him.'

She came down and the crone went up and called to the troops. They came and killed the horse that it might not speak to Yannaki, then caught and bound the fairest in the world. The crone goes up, takes Yannaki's sword, goes where he lay sleeping, deals him a blow and kills him. Then she called to the soldiers, who cut him into three hunks and cut the horse into another three hunks, then dug a large pit and threw the hunks in there. They threw in the brogues and the cap as well, shoved everything there together, tossed Yannaki's sword into the sea and then took away the fairest in the world, locked up the tower and went to the royal palace. The crone went with them.

The king rejoiced greatly. He granted the crone half his kingdom, placed the fairest in the world in a room made of gold, had handmaidens and ladies-in-waiting attend her and would visit her every morning. She would have none of him: neither wanted she to see him, nor to hear him. All she did was weep piteously.

But let us leave the princess to her woe and let us go to Yannaki's three brothers. Each had gone on living in bliss with his wife in his kingdom.

One morning as the sun's son awakened he went to look at the apple that Yannaki had left with him; he wanted to find out how his brother was faring. The apple was all wrinkled up! Its leaves were yellow and withered!

He went directly to his wife and said to her, 'My brother Yannaki has met with some misfortune. I must leave you and seek him.'

He mounted his horse and rode off. He went and found the other two brothers. The three of them set out on their quest together, and on and on they went... and they asked after him all along the way. Nobody knew where Yannaki might be.

Said the sun's son, 'I know what we need to do. Let us ask my father.'

They asked the sun and he said to them, 'You will go to such and such a place, you will get to the tower, you will dig the soil and you will find him.'

Off they went, dug, found Yannaki and the horse and matched the hunks together, but they didn't have the undying water.

They asked the sun again, and he said to them, 'All day, when I'm about, it's never happened that I've seen it. Ask the moon, perhaps it has seen it during the night.'

The moon's son went and asked the moon, and the moon said, 'Yes, I do know where it is. It's behind the mountain that clashes open and shut. Tie a little flagon onto a pigeon's leg and let the pigeon go and dip in it and collect the water and manage to come out before the mountain clashes shut.'

They attached the flagon to the pigeon's leg and it flew and passed through into the heart of the mountain. And it brought back the undying water.

They took the water, sprinkled Yannaki with it, sprinkled the horse and they revived! Rejoicing, hugs, embraces...

Said Yannaki, 'Thank you, my brothers, for you have been my saviours. Now I need to find my sword and kill all those who stole my wife and did me this great evil.'

They set off, all three, and the sun's son asked his father. Said the sun, 'I do not see it. I know not where it is.'

The moon's son asked the moon, who said, 'I have not seen it.'

The sea's son asked his mother. She said, 'I have it.'

The sea's son dived into his mother's bosom, searched for it and found it. He took it and brought it to Yannaki.

Yannaki thanked his brothers once again. They embraced and then they separated, each going back to his kingdom and his wife.

Yannaki mounted his horse, bent over its ear, fondled it and spoke, 'Come, let's go now, my good steed, to set our mistress free!'

The horse sprang forward and in two shakes it was outside the king's palace. The moment the soldiers saw Yannaki they were aghast! However could it be that he was alive again? They had buried him themselves, and they had seen him slain!

They made to block his way at the gate, lest he should enter. He drew his sword, swung it this way once, swung it that way once and he killed them all. He went into the palace and killed the king. He found the crone and chopped her up into tiny little pieces. He went to the rooms his wife was kept in and grabbed hold of her. They mounted the horse and rode off to their tower.

With the enchantments she was versed in, the fairest in the world spirited the tower away once again, along with the boughs of gold. She removed it from the world and brought it to the place where it had ever been. And that's where they lived the two of them, she and Yannaki, happy and filled with love for one another. Perhaps they are living there still for all I know.

Sun and Moon

Once there was an old man and an old woman. The old man went to his vineyard with his hoe to turn the soil and found himself before the sun and the moon in the middle of an argument.

When they saw the old man they said, 'Well met, Gramps. Tell us, do you know which one of us is the better of the two? The sun or the moon? Which of us do you find the better of the two? Who's the one that most befits this world?'

Then the old man said, 'The sun befits the day and the moon befits the night.'

So they were well pleased, both the sun and the moon, and they asked the old man what he would have them give him in return for such a fair pronouncement.

'Whatever you like you can give me,' said the old man. 'I am content as it is.'

So the sun and the moon produced a hen and gave it

to the old man and told him that, once he had travelled half the way, or even further, he should command the hen, 'Hen, lay me a fistful of florins' and she would. And whenever he told her to she would lay him florins.

The old man took the hen with him, and once he had reached half the way and a bit beyond, he commanded her, 'Lay me a fistful of florins, hen,' and the hen laid him the florins.

Joyfully, the old man went home and told the old woman of the stroke of luck that had fallen upon them in their old age. Then the old man went to find a handyman to build a silver chicken coop for the hen, and exhorted the old woman to refrain from divulging the attributes of the hen to him.

So the handyman arrived and set to building the chicken coop.

The old woman was of a rather boastful nature, and she sat down with the handyman and told him that her hen could lay florins. She was utterly unable to keep a secret; she couldn't even hold on to a dried broad bean should her life depend on it. She went so far as to command the hen, 'Hen, lay me a fistful of florins', right there in the handyman's presence, and the hen did so.

Seeing that, the handyman, who was cunning, took another hen from the yard outside, one that looked quite a bit like the good one and, surreptitiously, as he was erecting the chicken coop, put the dud hen inside it and, without anyone being any the wiser, stole the good hen that could lay florins.

The old couple fed the dud hen, thinking she was the good one. They had no clue that the handyman had played a dirty trick on them!

Some few days later the old man had need of a bit of cash. He caught hold of the hen and said to her, 'Hen, lay me a fistful of florins.' Then the hen relieved herself, depositing some droppings in the old man's hand. The old man was revolted and ready to be sick. He went and washed, and rushed off to beg the handyman to give him back his hen.

He said to him, 'Brother, now what's done is done. You know our secret too. I beg of you, give me back the hen, and whatever she lays we'll go half and half.'

That handyman was a bad egg though and he drove the poor old man away, saying, 'Never seen you, never knew you. I know nothing of what you're spouting at me. Off with you. Be gone.'

The poor old man went home dejected and sat there musing on the handyman's nastiness. Then he took hold of his hoe and went to his vineyard to turn the soil.

As he was on his way, once again he found before him the sun and the moon having it out, and they asked him who should enjoy precedence, who was superior in worth.

Then the old man said, 'The sun graces the day and the moon adorns the night.'

They were most gratified again, the two of them, and asked him what he would like them to give him in reward.

'Whatever is your pleasure, my dears,' he said.

They produced a tablecloth, gave it to him and said, 'When you've gone halfway, spread this tablecloth and you will find on it whatever you desire. So eat your fill and whenever you want to eat, spread the tablecloth and you will find whatever you fancy there. But watch out it doesn't happen that they take the tablecloth away from you.'

'Never fear,' said the old man. 'Now I've learnt my lesson and I will trust nobody.'

Then the old man took the tablecloth away with him and set forth, travelled half the way and spread the tablecloth and found on it everything he fancied, and sat down there and ate.

Then he went on home, replete and in good spirits, and he sat and told the old woman how fortunate they were now in their old age. Then they spread the tablecloth and sat down and ate and drank as much as they felt like.

That's what they did every day, and they were content as content can be, because in this way they had no need either of working or of spending money. Whatever they desired to eat they could have, and they wanted for nothing.

One day said the old man to the old woman, 'Let us invite the king with his troops and treat him from this tablecloth and make him wonder at this bounty!'

'You speak rightly, old man,' said the old woman. 'This is a fine idea. Let us do as you say, and see then in what great regard the king shall hold us.'

So the old man invited the king to come to his house, along with his troops, in order that they might be his guests.

The king was astonished on hearing such an invitation, but lest he put the old man in a resentful mood, he readied himself and his army and went to visit the old man at his house.

When he got there the old man spread the tablecloth and invited the king to eat of whatever he fancied. (I wish you'd been there, somehow, to see the manner in which there arose from the tablecloth all sorts of viands and sweetmeats and delicacies and wondrous old vintages.) When the king had eaten his fill, and his troops had too, he asked the old man how he had come by this tablecloth, and the man didn't want to give the truth away, and spouted all sorts of fibs: that he had found it one day in his vineyard as he had been turning the soil.

Then the king said to him, 'Old man, you've no business with such a tablecloth. This should go to me, who has this large army to feed. You have no children, nor any dogs; there's just the two of you boneheads, and you've no need of such a thing.'

And the king removed the tablecloth and carried it away, and didn't even turn his head to heed the wails of the old man and the old woman.

The poor old man wept and wept and then, somehow, he found solace, took up his pitchfork and went out to toil in his vineyard as had been his wont of old.

As he was on his way, the sun and the moon appeared before him, having an altercation as usual, for they knew not which of them was superior.

Once again they asked the old man and he said to them, 'The sun is worthy of the day, and the moon is worthy of the night.'

Then they brought out a sturdy wooden club, handed it to the old man and said to him, 'Let it not come about that you should tell this club "Don't you bash, club," for then you'll get to know about it.'

The old man took the club and once he'd reached half the way he wanted to get a measure of the might of the club and he said to it, 'Don't you bash, club.'

Directly the club started bashing him on his back and would almost have smashed his head. The poor old man fell to beseeching it, and it was all he could do to get the club to let him be.

Later on, when he arrived home, he got to thinking about how he could get back both the hen and the tablecloth with the prowess of the club.

So he went to visit the handyman who had filched his hen and said to him, 'Let me have my hen back.'

'Never knew you,' said he, 'never seen you.'

So the old man said to the club, 'Club, don't you bash him.'

At this the club started bashing the handyman, and had him all black and blue with the beating. The handyman was truly frightened then and brought out the hen and handed it over. The old man took it and carried it back home and put it in the silver chicken coop.

Then he went to the king and said to him, 'My king, enough is enough! You've held on to my tablecloth most unlawfully for ever so long. You have no right to it, so let me have it back now.'

The king said, 'Get lost. Be gone with you at once or I shall give orders to my troops and they'll come and slay you.'

Then the old man said to the club, 'Club, don't you bash the king.'

And the club began bashing the king ruthlessly and would have dispatched him. The king panicked and brought the tablecloth and handed it to the old man. On receiving it, the old man went back home and sat down happily with his old woman, and they ate and drank their fill nicely, and since then nobody could or did bother them again, and they've been living fine and dandy and we've been living better still.

The Almond Tree and the Cicada

One day a poor man was walking in his neighbourhood, returning from a weaver, and at his workshop he saw a black hen tied with red twine. When he got home he heard his neighbour crying that her black hen had been taken from her and that retribution from God should fall on them that did it, and suchlike.

He called out to her and said, 'If you give me two crowns I'll show you where the hen is.'

So she promised, and after he pretended to consult some books, he said to her, 'I've found her! She is at such and such a workshop, so run along and get her.'

She ran there, found her hen and gave him the two crowns.

Then his own wife said to him, 'This looks like a fine occupation; you could be a diviner.'

And he resolved to be a diviner and pronounce divinations.

As he was sitting at a crossroads one day the king's servants passed by and asked him whether the queen would give birth to a girl or a boy.

And, because he knew not what to tell them, he pretended to be reading a book and kept muttering, 'A boy, a girl, a boy, a girl . . .'

And they got tired of listening to his rambling, and continued on their way.

But it came to pass that when the queen gave birth she bore a boy and a girl, twins. The servants then recalled the diviner and said to the king what he had said to them.

In those days the king's strongbox had been stolen and, when the king heard of the diviner, he sent for him, and had him brought along with much pomp and circumstance, with troops, with royal music.

The poor diviner was atremble with trepidation, but what was there for him to do. How was he to know who it was that had made away with the strongbox!

A day passed, two days, three days, nothing doing. Of an evening he asked for a dish of almonds to be brought to him and he kept cracking them open and munching on them.

The thieves, there were three of them. One was outside the door and was standing in readiness to see whether the diviner would guess aright.

After he had eaten plenty of almonds, the diviner felt drowsy and said, 'Here is the first one.' (A bout of sleep is what he meant.)

The thief standing outside heard those words and was frightened. He went to the others and said to them, 'Hey comrades, the diviner is on to us. I was outside his room and heard him say, "Here is the first one".'

But they didn't believe him, and the second one went and stood behind the door.

The diviner woke up and started cracking almonds again and munching them. He felt drowsy once more and said, 'Here is the second one.'

The thief heard and went to tell the others.

'He sensed me too,' he said to them. 'I went there also, and heard him say "Here is the second one".'

The third one went to see for himself.

The soothsayer awoke again and he cracked some almonds and munched on them. Again he felt drowsy and said, 'And this one makes three.' (He meant the third bout of sleep, of course.)

So the third thief also went and said to the others, 'That devil of a diviner is on to us.'

Then they all went and knocked on the diviner's door, and they said to him, 'We know you're a proper sorcerer and have sniffed out all three of us, but look here, please don't go and betray us to the king, and in return we'll show you where the strongbox lies.'

They took him along and showed him.

Several days went by. The king asked him, 'Hey, diviner, have you any idea at all?'

'Yes, I've got some idea,' he said. 'Let me have a servant to help me dig.'

The king gave him a servant. They went to a place in the garden, dug and found the strongbox intact, full of florins, and the king was pleased and showered all sorts of gifts on him. And after they had their meal together, he took him with him and they went out into the garden.

As they walked around, the king grabbed a cicada in his hand from one of his almond trees and said to him, 'If you be a true diviner let's see what you shall tell me now. What am I holding in my hand here?'

The poor diviner, whose name was Tzitziras (meaning cicada), while his wife was called Mygdalia (almond tree), in his fright and terror blurted out the following words, 'A fine thing for you, Tzitziras, that Mygdalia should let you fall into the king's hands!'

The king took him to be talking about the cicada he was holding in his hand and the almond tree whence he had picked it up, and was overjoyed and gave him much gold, and so the man went back home at last and lived well, nay, even better than well.

The Papadia and Her Firewood

Neighbours would come and beg for the firewood that the priest had chopped.

'Give us a bit of firewood, papadia,' and the papadia, the priest's wife, would let them take some away.

The priest said to her, 'Papadia, don't give the firewood away. To chop it and to fetch it is quite some chore.'

'Whatever do you mean?' said the papadia. 'It's just plain old wood!'

And she kept giving it away to all comers who would ask for some.

When they had run out: 'Now, papadia, you fetch the firewood,' said the priest to her.

'Well, alright then, and why not?'

So the papadia did go, in fact, and it was sheer murder to chop the firewood and fetch it.

Came the neighbours: 'A bit of firewood, papadia...'

'Oh no, you don't,' she said. 'Now the firewood is the papadia's.'

But so long as the priest had been chopping the wood it had been worth nothing.

The Eggs

In those times there was a ship and its master. One day the master had sailed into a port and looked about for an inn, for a bite to eat.

He found one, walked in and asked the innkeeper, 'Is there any food left for me to have?'

'I'm out of everything, you poor fellow! All the dishes I'd cooked are finished. The one thing I do have is three or four fried eggs. Will that do? Shall I put them before you for you to eat?'

The ship's master agreed and sat down and began eating.

As he was eating there came in one of his sailors, who said that the anchors were dragging because a strong wind had blown up!

The skipper left off his meal and rushed to his ship. He boarded her forthwith, and weighed the anchors, but still they couldn't secure the ship. However, God and St Nicholas came to their aid and the ship was spared the worst in that tempest.

It took five or six years before the ship called at that port again.

When he came there the master went to pay for his eggs, for the matter had been weighing on him. He hadn't forgotten he was owing the debt.

The innkeeper produced a bill that was incalculable.

'Those eggs, if I'd let them be brooded by the hen, they would have hatched four birds: two cockerels, two hens.'

He took him to court, because with this and with that, and those eggs becoming fowl... He'd take his ship and he still wouldn't have discharged his debt.

The man went this way and that in dread of the prospect of losing his ship over four eggs! He came to another inn where elderly menfolk preferred to go. There he found a lawyer of sorts.

The lawyer saw that the man was distressed, found out about his case and sat next to him and told him, 'Captain, treat me to a drink of wine and do not fret. I will save your ship, come tomorrow.'

The captain had a cup of wine brought for the lawyer immediately. The lawyer drank and directly composed a brief, which he took to the court. The brief appointed himself as the captain's counsel in the case.

The following day dawned. It turned nine o'clock, it turned ten o'clock, then eleven o'clock; it was getting close to noon. Everybody with court business had gathered, but our lawyer had not yet made his appearance.

At about quarter to twelve he was seen far off and approaching! He was humming along the way.

Said the judge, 'A fine job, my good man! You've kept us waiting all this time long, and we are famished!'

'Ach, brother, lay off me! Yesterday I got me two pecks of broad beans and sent them home to my wife. She baked them all in one go. We'd been eating all day long yesterday, and some in the morning today, and still there were plenty left over. So I went to sow them and that made me late for the hearing.'

The innkeeper cut in and asked him, 'But do baked broad beans sprout?'

The lawyer responded and said, 'Do cooked eggs hatch birds?'

Without any further ado our lawyer cut to the chase, pronouncing: 'Captain, you've eaten four eggs. That's four thruppenny bits plus tuppence for the bread. That's a shilling and tuppence. Give him that and he can go about his business.'

The judge concurred and the captain retained his boat. In gratitude, the captain gave some cash to the innkeeper so he would serve the lawyer wine for as long as the cask hadn't been drained of its contents.

Three Pieces of Good Advice

There was once a poor man whose name was Yannis, and all he had was his wife and a ten-year-old child. Every day the man worked from dawn till dusk for a mere pittance, hardly enough to feed his family a crust of bread.

One day Yannis said to his wife, 'This sort of life is just unbearable, woman. You can see for yourself that I work like a dog from morning till dusk and there's nothing left to show for it. I'll take my eyes along with me and leave. I will take me to foreign parts to find me a decent job and I'll send you some money for you to make do properly, together with our child.'

'You go then, and may you fare well, my man,' said his wife. 'Just don't forget your hearth, and do send us a little something so we can get by.'

So Yannis left his village and went to the city, but he couldn't find any really decent job for he was unschooled, and was forced to take up employment as a retainer for a well-to-do burgher.

This master, no matter how many years Yannis worked for him, did not pay him as much as a farthing.

Only the master's wife would give him a coin every now and then, and he sent that on to his village, to his wife.

Ten years had passed and Yannis was fed up with being away from home and yearned to go back to his village, to his wife and his child. His heart ached to return home.

He readied his things and said to his master that he should be getting paid his wages, all the money that was owing to him for his pains and his service.

His master brought out three florins and said, 'Here, Yannis. Take these here florins. Over the ten years you were in my employ that is what your work amounted to in worth. Take these coins then and be off with you, and fare you well.'

Poor old Yannis took the three florins, realized this was not nearly enough, but said nothing. He just sighed under his breath, bid his master goodbye and started on the way to his village.

When he was already some way off his master called him back and said, 'Yannis, give me back one florin, and I'll give you a piece of advice.'

'But, master, I don't…'

'No, give it to me,' he said.

What was Yannis to do? He handed it over.

His master said to him, 'Ask no questions about such as is none of your business.'

'Alright,' said Yannis, and made a move to be off.

He hadn't as much as quit the gate and his master called him back again.

'Come here! Come here! Give me one more florin and I'll give you another piece of advice.'

Yannis gave back one more coin.

The master says to him, 'Never veer off the path you've embarked on.'

Yannis started on his way again and he mused, and said to himself, 'What am I to do, poor old me, with just one florin? How can I go back home with just a single florin after ten years in foreign parts?'

He hadn't put much distance between him and the house when his former master called him for the third time.

'Give me that other florin too, and I'll give you one more piece of advice.'

He took back the florin and said to him:

'Tonight's wrath,

hold it until morn!'

So, penniless and miserable, Yannis left for his village. On the road as he was travelling he saw a Moor who was atop a tree and was gluing florins onto the tree's leaves. It seemed bizarre, but he didn't say anything to the Moor because he remembered the first piece of advice he had been given by his master, and so he kept going straight ahead.

'Hey, man, stop you right there!' the Moor called out.

Yannis stopped fearfully, and the Moor said to him, 'I've been at this for one hundred years, sitting here on this tree and doing what you saw me doing. There's been all sorts of people passing by and they all stopped in their tracks and asked me why I was gluing the florins onto the leaves, and I ate them all. It's only you that didn't ask me, but kept going along your way. Well done! You are a very wise man. Well done! I'm giving you all these coins because you deserve them. Here you are. You are worthy to have them. Now you be on your way again, and fare you well.'

Yannis took the coins, filled his pockets and the inside of his shirt and continued on, elated.

He kept thinking along the way, and was saying to himself, 'In truth, it was really well worth a florin, this first piece of advice my master gave me.'

After three days on the road he happened to meet some muleteers driving some thirty laden mules. They were going the same way. Yannis begged them for a ride for part of the way for he was tired. So they all kept going on that road.

After a while they came to an inn, and the muleteers went inside to have a cup or two of wine and invited Yannis to go along with them. But he remembered the second piece of advice his master had given him, never to veer from the path he had embarked on, so he didn't go along with them. He stayed outside and kept the mules from running away. And then, as the muleteers were drinking their wine in the inn, there was a mighty earthquake and the inn collapsed and crushed all those in it, the innkeeper and the muleteers too.

Yannis was right frightened by the earthquake but he came to no harm. He made the sign of the cross on his person and thought, 'That second piece of advice my master gave me was definitely worth the florin I paid him.'

Getting the mules to go along with him, laden with goods as they were, he resumed his way.

After he'd travelled several more days he reached his village. He made directly for his house, with the mules. He knocked on the door. His wife opened it, but she didn't know him. He did not reveal who he was; he only asked her to let him spend the night there in the yard along with his mules.

She said to him, 'If you'd asked me to put you up in the house, I wouldn't have let you in, but you can spend the night out there with your mules as the wayfarer that you are. There is also this shed adjoining the yard, and if you like you can prepare your bedding and sleep under its shelter.'

Not long after, as he was tending to the mules, he saw a man pass through and step into the house.

'Oh! My wife must have remarried,' he thought, 'and she's forgotten all about me.'

Yannis was sore over this, and he grabbed his rifle to go in and kill them, both him and her. But he remembered his master's third piece of advice: tonight's wrath, hold it until morn. So he laid his gun aside and lay down, but there was no sleep for him!

In the morning, when it grew light, Yannis got up and set out some barley for the mules. The family had arisen and Yannis heard the man who had entered the house the night before say to his wife, 'Mother, I'll be off now, and come noon I'll be sending you some beans to cook.'

Then he smacked his head with both his hands at the thought that he had almost killed his child, and he rushed in and revealed himself to his wife and child. They hugged and kissed, and he set out the merchandise he'd carried with the mules and, with the florins too that he'd brought, they had a fine time of it and we a finer one yet.

Poulia and Avgerinos[4]

Beginning of the tale,
good evening to you gentlefolk.

Once upon a time there was a hunter and his wife. And one fine day his wife gave birth to a pretty girl and they named her Poulia. But not much later the woman died, and the hunter —what else could he do?—he remarried.

The second wife, Poulia's stepmother we could call her, also gave birth—to a little boy and they named him Avgerinos.

As Poulia was growing up, the stepmother grew envious and wanted to sell her off as a slave, and she spoke of that in secret to her husband. Avgerinos heard what his mother was saying, and went and told Poulia.

---

4 The Pleiades and the Morning Star.

'My dearest Poulia, my mother will sell you into slavery. What should we do now?'

Poulia went to visit an old granny who was their neighbour to ask for advice, you ken.

And the old neighbour said to her, 'You need to flee my girl. Get out of her clutches. As she combs your hair for the bazaar, Avgerinos will pull the ribbon from your hair and you will run after him and that is how you'll escape. Your stepmother will run after you to catch you and you'll throw this knife and there will appear a plain without any edges. But your stepmother will cross it fast and she will reach you. Then you'll toss this comb and it will turn into a dense thicket of thorns and brambles, but she will cross that too and she will gain on you. Then you'll scatter this here salt and it will turn into a wide lake that your stepmother won't be able to cross, and she'll have to turn back.' So she handed a knife, a comb and the salt to the children and sent them off.

When the children arrived back home the stepmother set to combing Poulia's hair, and she sang to her and kept telling her a whole lot of falsehoods. Then Avgerinos grabbed the ribbon from Poulia's plait and ran out, and Poulia ran after him, and they were out on the road. The stepmother ran behind them to catch up with them. Then Poulia tossed away the old woman's knife and it became a plain with no edges. But the stepmother crossed the plain in two shakes and almost managed to reach the children. But Poulia tossed the old woman's comb and it turned into a dense thicket of thorns and brambles. The stepmother crossed that too and then Poulia scattered the salt and it became a huge lake. The stepmother sought to cross it but how? Then she hurled a curse upon Avgerinos, who was her child, mind you, but who had repudiated his mother and sided with her stepdaughter.

'There where you're going,' she said, 'when you are thirsty and drink water, whatever animal's footprint you may drink from, such shall you become!'

When they had reached some far distant spot, Avgerinos said, 'I'm thirsty, Poulia!'

'Keep walking,' said she to him, 'and over there is the king's fountain and you may drink then.'

They kept going and covered some considerable distance, and the child said, 'I'm so thirsty; I can't go any further.'

And there he found a wolf's footprint filled with water and said to her, 'I'll drink from here.'

'Don't drink,' said she, 'for you'll become a wolf and you shall eat me up.'

'Then I won't drink if that's the way it is!' and they set off again.

On and on they went, on and on, and they found a sheep's footprint filled with water, and the child said to her, 'I'll drink from here. I can't hold off any longer; I'm desperate.'

'Don't drink,' said Poulia to him, 'for you'll become a sheep and they'll have you butchered.'

'I'll drink,' he said, 'and let them have me butchered.'

And he drank and turned into a sheep and he ran after her, bleating.

'Baa Poulia, baa Poulia!'

'Come close to me,' said Poulia.

Poulia went ahead and behind her came the sheep, Avgerinos, and they went on and on, and they reached the king's fountain. Poulia drew some water and gave the sheep some to drink and drank some herself.

And by the fountain was a cypress, ever so tall, and Poulia beseeched God, 'Almighty God, please give me the strength to climb to the top of this cypress!'

And the moment she was done praying she found herself atop the cypress, and high up where she sat became a throne of gold and the sheep stayed under the cypress and kept on grazing.

Some time later there appeared the servants of the king to water the horses and, as they neared the cypress, the horses started and snapped their halters and stepped away from the rays emanating from Poulia, who shone refulgent from high up on the cypress.

'Come down,' said the servants to her, 'for the horses are frightened and won't drink water.'

'I'm not coming down,' she said to them. 'Let the horses drink their water. I'm not bothering any of you.'

'Come on down,' they said again.

'I'm not coming down.'

So they went to the prince and told him about it: 'Near the spring, high up on the cypress there sits a maiden and her beauty shines brightly, and the horses are affrighted of her radiance and they refuse to drink and we told her to come down, but she doesn't wish to.'

On hearing this the prince got up and went there and said to her that she should come down. But she didn't wish to. And he said it to her a second time and then a third.

'Come on down for we shall fell the cypress if you don't climb down.'

'Fell it,' she said. 'I'm not coming down.'

So he got men to cut the cypress down and, while they were axing it, the sheep went and licked the cypress and it grew to double the size it had been. They laboured at it and laboured at it, but they just couldn't bring it down.

'Get away with you all,' said the prince, full of wrath.

And so they all went away. Then, to give vent to his frustration, he went to an old crone and said to her, 'If you bring me that girl down from the cypress I shall fill your headscarf full of florins.'

'I will get her down for you,' said the crone.

And she got hold of a trough and a sieve and some flour and went beneath the cypress and put the trough upside down, as well as the sieve, and that's how she sieved the flour. The girl saw this from high up in the cypress and raised a big fuss.

'Turn them the right way up, old woman—the trough and the sieve too.'

The crone pretended to be hard of hearing, and said,

'I can't hear you my poppet. Climb down a wee bit.' And she kept on sieving the wrong way.

'Turn them the right way up, old woman—the trough as well as the sieve,' said Poulia a second time, and then a third.

And the old woman said to her again, 'I can't hear you, my poppet. Come on down and show me, and may all of God's blessings be with you.'

And so the maiden came down little by little, and when she went to show the crone the prince stepped out from his hiding place and grabbed hold of her, and put her on his saddle and off they went.

The poor sheep that had been grazing down there, beneath the cypress, started bleating away and Poulia started wailing.

'My lamb, my poor lambkin!'

The prince said to her then, 'Don't worry, I can bring you as many sheep as you like,' but Poulia would hear none of it.

'I won't give away my own darling sheep for anything in the world,' she said to him.

What else could the prince do? He gave orders and they brought the sheep to the room in the palace, and then the prince married Poulia.

The king had great love for his daughter-in-law, but the queen became furiously jealous of her and one day, when the prince was away hunting, she took her daughter-in-law along with her to promenade, or so she said, in the grounds. And as they were going round they came to a dry well. The mother-in-law gave Poulia a shove and threw her into the well.

The sheep sensed it and began bleating, and the mother-in-law, in order to silence its mouth too, sought to slaughter it.

When the prince returned and didn't see Poulia there, he asked his mother, 'Mother, where is my bride?'

'Outdoors,' said she. 'She's gone out for a walk. And it's a good thing too that she isn't here now for we can have the sheep slaughtered!'

The sheep heard all that, and ran to the well and said to Poulia, 'Poulia, they will have me slaughtered!'

'Hush, my darling eyes! They won't do that.'

'There, they're whetting their blades; they've caught me! They'll slaughter me!'

Then the queen's serving maids caught the sheep and set about to butcher it, and as they brought their knife to its neck, Poulia beseeched God and said, 'My God! They are killing my brother and here am I stuck in this well!'

In a flash she was out of the well, and she rushed to find the sheep, whose throat they'd already slit. She wailed, and cried that they should let it go. But it had already had its throat slit.

'My darling sheep,' she moaned, and she wailed, and she cried, 'My sheep!' There was no comforting her.

The poor prince promised her as many sheep as there were in the world. She wouldn't have it.

'My sheep, my darling sheep!' she kept wailing all the while.

And with this, and with that, they had the sheep roasted and served it at table.

'Come, let us eat,' they said.

'I've already eaten,' she said. 'I'm not eating anything else now.'

'Do come, dear. Come and eat,' they said to her.

'You eat. I tell you I've already eaten.'

And when they had finished eating she went and gathered all the bones and put them in a jar, which she buried in the garden.

In the morning, at that spot, they saw rearing up an orange tree, high and huge, with a gold orange at its very top.

On seeing it the gorgon of a mother-in-law started yelling, 'I want the orange; I want that orange!'

But since nobody could reach it she took it on herself to bring the orange down. Then the branches turned upon her and put her eyes out.

Poulia saw from where she was and said, 'Let me try to bring it down.' As she drew close, the orange descended and said to her, 'Hold me tight, Poulia,' and as she held it there was a thunderclap and she rose high up into the sky and she said, 'Fare well, my kind father-in-law, and you my kind prince. I cannot live in this world: from the hands of the wicked stepmother I fell into the hands of the evil mother-in-law.'

And ever since then they have been two luminaries up in the night sky, the Pleiades and the morning star.

The Poor, Kind Child

Once upon a time there was a very poor woman and she had four children, all girls. She worked hard in order to raise them, the poor thing, but whatever should she attend to first? A day's wages are spent in a day. All she earned was barely enough to buy her children bread. She had them going around naked and unshod; there wasn't any money left over to buy them anything by way of clothes. Once in a while some charitable Christian lady might give her some cast-off, and she'd alter it for her eldest first, then take it in for her second or her third girl. There was never anything for the littlest one who, winter or summer, had to go about in just a shift reduced to rags, unshod and her poor neck all bare.

Then a year came when winter was extra harsh! Rain, frost, snows. The poor mite was shivering and couldn't warm herself. She said to her mother, 'Mother! I'm going to leave! I need a mother who can make me something to wear for once. If I stay on here I will surely die! In just this tattered shift I'll soon perish!'

The child left! On she went... on she went... On the road she found a little bird beneath a tree. It was tiny and featherless. It had fallen out of its nest and was chirping in shock. It hadn't the strength to fly up to its nest on the branches overhead. It would soon perish down there on the ground.

The child took pity on it. She took it in her hands and warmed it in her palms. She looked around and then she saw a man coming along and she asked him to put it back in its nest. She'd saved the bird!

The child resumed her path and was about to pass through a copse. But she saw a spider weaving her silk up and down, back and forth, making her web broader all the while, as if she were in a great hurry. The child brought herself up short and said to herself, 'Let me not ruin her weaving. Let me go the other way lest I cause grief to that poor spider.'

Said the spider to her, 'Thank you, kind child! For this kindness of yours what would you like me to do in return? Where are you off to, all bare and unshod?'

'I'm off to find some cloth to take it to my mother for her to sew me something to put on, for I am shivering with cold.'

'Go,' said the spider, 'and on your return stop by here again to tell me of the outcome of your quest, and I'll help you so far as I can.'

The child continued on her way and came to a clump of brambles. She tried to pass through it, but her shift got caught in the thorns and was reduced to tatters and the child was left naked. She was in tears. It would have broken your heart to hear her and to see her so.

A little lamb was grazing there, further down in a meadow, and heard the child.

It said to her, 'What is the matter, my child? Why are you crying? Did somebody beat you?'

'Oh!' said the child. 'I was looking to find me some clothes to put on, and I passed here and the brambles tore my shift to tatters, and now I'm stark naked.'

The lamb asked the brambles, 'Well, why ever did you cause her such harm? What'll happen to the child now?'

'Let's have some of your wool and we'll card it. She can take it then and bring it to her mother, and she can make clothes of it, woollen ones that are warm, so she won't go cold,' said the brambles.

So the lamb went round and round the brambles and left its wool on the thorns, and the child gathered it, all nicely carded and ready.

Once she had gathered enough, she said, 'Thank you, my dear lamb! Now I'll be off to get to my mother quickly, so she can spin it and weave it, cut it and sew it before Christmas so I can put it on when I go to receive communion.'

The child sped along the road joyfully, but was thinking too that her mother might not be able to finish all these tasks in good time, seeing that she was jobbing for her wages, and that worried her somewhat.

When she reached the tree holding the bird's nest, there before her she found the bird's mother.

'Ah, kind child!' she said to her. 'How to thank you? The kindness you did to me in saving my little bird...

How shall I repay you? What's this that you are holding in your hands?'

Said then the child that it was the wool the lamb had given her and she was hurrying back to her mother to have her spin it, weave it, cut it, sew it and make some clothes for her, so she could have a dress to wear for Christmas and receive communion.'

'Give it to me. I'll spin it for you!' said the bird.

It took hold of it in its beak, flew high up, as high is high, and produced a length of yarn ever so long. Before one had time to turn and look, it was spun already and all rolled up into a ball!

The child took the ball and was off.

When she reached the spider, she was there waiting for her.

'Hello there! How have you managed? Have you found anything useful?'

On seeing the ball of yarn she held in her hand, the spider took the yarn and began to weave it without further ado, and it came out nice and smooth and sheer!

The child arrived back with her mother and gave her the stuff. Her mother cut out a little frock and sewed it, and the child put it on and looked nicely fitted out. She went to church and all lavished compliments on her, pretty, warm and nicely dressed as she looked.

Music Makers

Once upon a time there was a farmer and he had a donkey. The donkey had grown old and the farmer put him out and left him tied to a post in the open to die.

A hunter was passing by, and he had a hound but didn't want to keep it anymore for it had grown old and had lost its nose for hares.

The hound stopped in its tracks and asked the donkey, 'What are you doing there, you poor old donkey?'

The donkey said, 'My master has tied me to this post to die, because I've grown old.'

'And my master has chased me off, because I no longer have a nose for hares.'

'Would you care to join me then, to go off somewhere else, and we can be music makers?'

'I would, and gladly,' said the hound.

So the donkey snapped its halter in two, and they took off.

Outside the village they found a yowling cat sitting on a ledge and holding a handkerchief to wipe away its tears.

The donkey said to it, 'What are you crying for, pussycat?'

'What am I crying for? I've grown old and can't see the mice any longer, and for that my mistress has chased me away.'

'We're off to become music makers. Would you care to join us, then?'

'That I will,' she said.

Now the hound said to the donkey, 'My legs have hardly the strength to walk, old boy.'

The donkey said to him, 'Climb onto my back then.'

The hound got onto the donkey's back and the cat mounted too, and they ambled along, astride the donkey.

On they went, and on they went, and they came to a country cottage. Perched atop a pillar, there was a cockerel and he was crowing.

The donkey said to him, 'Hey, rooster, what are you crowing for?'

'Alas,' said the cockerel, 'my master has guests joining him, and he plans to slaughter me.'

'Why don't you come along with us then? We're going to be music makers.'

The cockerel jumped atop the donkey too.

On they went, and on they went. They reached a coppice and dusk fell.

They said to the cat, 'Climb up onto a tall tree, pussycat, and look around. Is there any sort of fire burning anywhere around?'

The cat climbed up a tree and saw a light shining in the wood. There was a hut and in the hut was a gang of robbers. Just as the robbers were taking the cauldron with their meal off the fire, the donkey put his head in through the window and began braying—hee-haw; the dog—woof, woof; the cat—meow, meow; the cockerel—cock-a-doodle…

The thieves were quite startled. They thought the animals were fairies and goblins and they bolted.

The donkey and his companions went inside, ensconced themselves there and ate their fill.

Once they had eaten, the donkey went outdoors and rolled around, the dog sat by the door, the cat curled up next to the fireplace and the cockerel roosted on a branch in front of the hut.

As night fell, and our music makers were sleeping, said the chief robber to his henchmen, 'Which one of you is brave enough to go and have a look at what's going on over at the hut?'

'I'll go,' said one of them.

'Good. Off you go then.'

So he went there and walked in. The dog at the door didn't bother him. He saw the cat's eyes and he thought, 'Those are embers that are still alive.' He went up close to light the lamp with the embers, and the startled cat clawed at his face. He made to get out, but the dog grabbed him by his ankles. He got outside and the donkey started kicking him. And from its branch, the cockerel crowed, 'Cock-a-doodle! Catch him; catch him!'

He fled in an awful fright. When he came back, they asked him how things had gone.

'Forget about it,' he said. 'I tried to have a look in the fireplace: a witch scratched at my face with her claws. I backed out: another one grabbed me by the legs. I got out and a huge one fetched me a blow with a club and knocked me out, and there was another one screeching "Catch him; catch him".'

The robbers wouldn't even think of going back to that hut! The donkey, the dog, the cat, and the cockerel:

Would eat and would drink
But share none of it with us

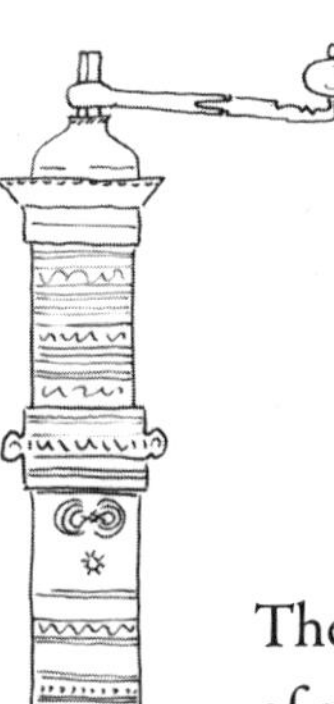

The Quern

There were two brothers once: one was a man of substance, the other poor. The former kept the latter as a shepherd.

Holy Saturday came round, and the rich man had to select the lambs that would be slaughtered for Easter. When they had sold most of the lambs, the poor brother begged the brother of substance for a small lamb to roast and share with his wife and children on Easter Sunday, the great holy day.

His brother, an avaricious soul you see, started an argument with him.

'You ingrate! Are you not happy that I keep you employed and I let you have your crusts of bread? Now you want a lamb too?'

The poor man spoke no more, save only after they had disposed of all the lambs and there was only a little scrawny one left unsold, so then he said to his brother, 'May I have this little one?'

'Take it,' he said, 'and be off with you to the demon's mother!'

The poor man was so upset at this that he resolved not to go home, not to go anywhere at all, only to take to the hills and the sticks and go to find 'the demon's mother'.

He ran as if he were demented. He went on, and went on, and he was overtaken by nightfall. He sat down to get his breath back and rest a little.

As he sat musing and ruminating, far off he saw a blaze. He got up again and went towards the light to see what it might be. He came close to the blaze, and what do you think greeted his eyes? There was a huge table and there sat the temptations in rows with the demons, all gathered together, and they were feasting, eating and drinking.

When they saw him one of them said, 'Welcome, Uncle!'

Then another, 'Welcome, Uncle! How did it come about that you've chanced upon us? We've been sitting at this place for ages and ages, and there's never been anyone to visit us. What came over you that you've turned up here?'

Now all the demons were plying him with questions.

The man said, 'I don't want anything. It's just that my brother gave me this lamb and told me to go to the demon's mother, and I took the lamb with me, and I came along and that's how I found you.'

They offered him something to eat, but he didn't want anything.

They asked him, 'What would you like us to give you for the gift you've brought us?'

'Whatever your heart can bear to part with. You can give me that.'

They gave him a quern, of the kind they grind coffee with, and they told him that when the quern ground it would produce all sorts of things—piasters, florins, fine dishes, all kinds of goods—and they instructed him never to yield it to anybody, whatever they might offer him in exchange.

The man took it with him and came back home at night, on Holy Saturday.

Easter Sunday was dawning. The poor man's children were whimpering for having had no bread to eat, for having no clothes; they were bewailing their fate.

When their father arrived home he brought out the quern and turned it a little. He brought out loaves of bread, fine dishes, florins, clothes, everything one's heart might desire! They got up in the morning, dressed and went to church, and they arrived there full of joy and Easter spirit.

His brother saw them then, the children and the wife of his brother, looking entirely different, looking all decent and proper.

'There must be something fishy going on here,' he thought.

He went about it one way; he went about it another way. He asked the children, and asked them again, and he found out that his brother had a quern that brought out all that stuff. He went to the man himself and asked him; the man sought to deny it all.

'Come on now, own up. Your own children were the ones that told me.'

Willy-nilly, the poor man had to come out with the truth. And then his brother started wheedling and cajoling; he must be given the quern and in return he'd give his brother piasters galore, and would bequeath him all his riches and every asset that he owned.

The man agreed, but first he went to his house and turned the quern and filled a coffer with florins, and then he went to his brother and handed it over to him.

Now his brother found no pleasure in holding on to the quern in that village of theirs, but took it with him to bring to the city, so he could show it off to all and sundry.

As they were voyaging in a ship, they had need of some salt. So he set about turning the quern to obtain the salt. But the quern did not leave off. It went on turning and turning and producing salt, and more salt, and it filled the ship with salt, and the ship sank, and all in it were drowned!

The quern was removed by the devils (away with them!) who took charge of it once again, but now the poor brother had lots and lots of florins and he lived in plenty.

The Luckless Princess

Once upon a time there was a queen who had three daughters and there was no future for them. The queen was grief-stricken that all around the other maidens should find husbands, but her daughters, though they were princesses, were getting on in years with nary a prospect of getting married.

One day a beggarwoman came by the palace asking for alms. Seeing the queen downhearted she asked her what the matter was, and so the queen spoke of her heartache.

Then the beggarwoman said to her, 'Listen to me. During the night, when your daughters are asleep, go and spy on them. See how they sleep and let me know.'

The queen did so. At night she spied on her daughters and found that her eldest kept her hands by her head, the middle one had her hands crossed over her chest and the youngest one had them folded between her knees.

The following day, when the beggarwoman came round and asked, the queen described what she had seen.

Then the beggarwoman said to her, 'Listen to me, mistress queen. The one who keeps her hands folded in between her knees as she sleeps, she is the one who is ill-fated. It is her fate that is blocking the prospects of the other ones.'

When the beggarwoman had departed, the queen remained deep in thought.

'Listen here, Mother,' said her youngest daughter to her. 'Do not grieve. I heard it all and realize that it is I who stand as an obstacle to my two elder sisters, so they aren't getting married. Get me my dowry in florins, sew them into the hem of my skirt and then let me be on my way.'

The queen balked and wouldn't let her go, saying, 'Where are you going to, my child?' but her daughter wouldn't heed her. She got herself up in a nun's habit and set off after she had bid her mother goodbye.

As she was on the way out from the palace gates, behold, there were two suitors already, coming to seek her sisters' hands.

So on she went, poor luckless thing, and on she went, until she reached a certain town, come evening. There she knocked on a merchant's door and begged him to let her spend the night at his house. He invited her up to the reception rooms (his *piano nobile*), but she declined and said she preferred to stay on the ground floor.

So at night her fairy godmother (her fate, in other words) turned up and took to ripping up all the stuff and merchandise they kept stored there, turning it into tatters and making a shambles of the place, despite the girl's entreaties that she should desist. The fate would have none of it; in fact she threatened to tear *her* to bits as well.

At daybreak the merchant came down to enquire of the nun whether she had spent a restful night. When he saw the havoc in his stores, with everything destroyed and the place a shambles, he said to the girl, 'Oh, my lady nun! What is this evil you have caused me? You've ruined me! What is to become of me now?'

'Hush,' said she, 'be quiet,' and she unstitched her hem and brought out gold florins and said to him, 'Will these do?'

'Enough, yes, they're more than enough...'

And so she took her leave of him and started wending her way along the road stretching ahead of her.

On she went and on she went until nightfall, which found her at the house of a glassware merchant.

The same story all over. She asked to be put up on the ground floor and her fate turned up at night and left nothing intact.

The following day the merchant came down to enquire of the nun how she was, and he beheld the havoc. He gave vent to howls and imprecations, but once she had filled his hands, too, with her gold florins he subsided and let her go.

She kept going on the road stretching ahead of her, poor luckless thing, until she came to the royal palace of that domain. There she asked to see the queen, and begged her for employment.

The queen, who was a canny woman, realized that beneath the habit there was a high-born lady and so she asked her whether she knew how to embroider with seed pearls. The girl replied that she knew all about embroidering with seed pearls and so the queen took her on. But when the poor thing sat down to do her embroidery, the portraits with their personages descended from the walls and snatched at the pearls and tormented her and didn't give her a moment's peace.

The queen would see all this and she pitied the girl. Often, when her handmaids complained that, overnight, the crockery would shatter, and accused the girl of being the one smashing it, the queen said to them, 'Hush you now, hush now, for she's a princess and a right noble lady, but she is ill-fated, poor thing.'

And then one day the queen turned to the girl and said, 'Listen, my child, to what I have to tell you. This way that you're dealing with the matter, you won't ever be able to lead a proper life, with your fate hounding you so. You need to find a way for her to make out a new portion for you.'

'But what am I to do?' said the girl. 'What must I do for her to let me have a new portion?'

'Come, I will tell you. Do you see that lofty mountain there in the distance? That is where all the fates of the world reside. That is where their palaces are to be found, and that is the road you need to take. You go up there to the peak of the mountain and find your fate and hand her the loaf of bread that I shall give you, and you say to her, "My fate, who pronounced my portion, please give me a new one". Do not leave, no matter what she might do to you. Just see to it that she takes your bread in her hands.'

This then is what the princess did. She took the loaf of bread and started out on the way stretching ahead of her, her path before her, until she arrived at the top of the mountain. She rang at the gate to the garden, and it opened, and out came a beautiful lady, very elegantly turned out.

'Oh, you are not one of mine,' she said, and went back inside.

Shortly after, another one came out, just as lovely and alluring.

'I don't know you, my good girl,' she said, and went away.

Then another one turned up, and another one, and many there were that came out but not one of them knew her as theirs, until a scurvy scold, a fusty frump, a termagant showed up at the gate.

'What do you want with me, you stupid nincompoop? What do you think you are doing here?' she said to the princess. 'Be gone with you! Back away! Scram! I'll cut you to bits!'

The poor girl offered her the loaf of bread and said, 'My fate, who assigned me my portion, oh, let me have a new one, please do.'

'Get lost! Go back to your mother and tell her to give birth to you anew, and to put you to her teat, and lull you to sleep, and then you can come back here and I'll let you have a new portion.'

The other fates urged her, 'Give her a new portion, the poor thing whom you have put through such dreadful misery, though she be a princess. Pronounce a new future for her, a prospect she can look forward to.'

'Can't do that. Let her take off; away with her!'

At some point she took hold of the bread, threw it straight at her head and it rolled off and fell down to the ground.

The girl picked it up and offered it to her again, and said to her, 'Take it my good fate; take it and let me have my new portion.'

The fate kept pushing her away; she even threw stones at her.

To cut a long story short, however, what with the words uttered by one fate, what with those of another fate, what with the persistence of the girl who kept handing her the loaf, at one point that nasty, horrid fate felt obliged to say to her, 'Give it to me,' and she snatched it from her.

The girl stood before her, all aquiver for fear that she would throw it back at her, but the fate held on to it and spoke to her thus: 'Listen very closely to what I have to say! Take this ball of thread,' and with that she tossed a ball of silk at her, 'and you watch out now! Neither sell it, nor give it away as a gift. Only part with it when you're asked for it, against its weight and according to the scales. Now you go about your business.'

The girl took the ball of silk and went back to the queen. Nothing disturbed her any longer.

In the neighbouring kingdom the king was getting married, and the bride's gown was missing some silk, which had to match the brocade.

The people at the palace enquired everywhere in the hope they'd find something to fit their purpose. They heard that in the neighbouring kingdom there was a girl who had a ball of silk, so they went and begged her to bring the ball with her to the palace of the bride to see whether it matched the gown.

When they got there they set the ball beside the gown and found it to be exactly like it, utterly indistinguishable. They asked her then what she required for it, and she replied that it was not for sale, but that she would exchange it according to its weight. So they put it on a pair of scales and piled up the other dish with florins, but the scales would not budge. They kept adding more florins, to no avail.

Then the prince got onto the scales himself, and the silk was balanced out. So the prince said, 'Seeing that your silk weighs as much as I do, for us to get the ball you need to take me!'

And so it turned out. The prince married the princess, and there was great rejoicing, and they lived together happily, and we lived better still.

Wolf, Fox and Ass

There was once an ass, sturdy and well fed, grazing in a field. A fox happened to see him and her appetite was roused. She went to get the wolf.

'Come along with me to have a look at that there ass. A delectable morsel, wouldn't you say?'

The wolf went to have a look, and saw the ass, and that got him drooling.

'You know what we should do, wolf?' said the fox.

'What? You're a cunning one, you are.'

'Let's buy a boat and load it with olives and take the ass along with us as our able-bodied seaman, and when we are out at sea we can eat him. So, there you are. You get a boat and I'll strike a deal with the ass.'

So the wolf went and bought a boat, (remember, this *is* a fairy tale, after all) and loaded it with olives. The fox fetched the ass and they went down to the shore and boarded the boat.

Once they had reached the open sea, the fox said, 'All well and good! We are sailing on now, but who's to know if we'll come out of this alive! Why don't you come to make your confession, just in case?'

The wolf turned father confessor, and had the fox make her confession before anyone else.

'What sins have you been guilty of, madam fox?'

'I've nipped several chickens, and have eaten some other critters—hares, coneys, bunnies; there, that kind of creature did I kill and eat.'

'As if it wasn't your business, madam fox. Those are the lowliest of the earth that you've been eating. Come now, you hear my confession.'

'Tell me then—what sins have you been guilty of?'

'I've eaten several sheep, and several goats, and not a few heifers.'

'Ah, the lowliest of the low, the mere worms of this earth.'

Then the wolf turned to the ass.

'Come you now, sir ass, unburden yourself of your sins. What have you been guilty of?'

'There was that one day,' said the ass, 'when, loaded as I was with lettuces, my head turned around and my jaws tore off a leaf, for it looked so wonderfully luscious and delectable, and I ate it.'

'Fie, sir ass!' said they with one voice.

Alas, you have consumed the lettuce leaf
with neither vinegar, no, nor with oil.
How is it then we did not drown during this,
our voyage, and in an awful turmoil!

'Your sin is most grievous, and therefore we must eat you.'

'Oh, woe is me.'

'No, but we must eat you.'

'Alright,' said the ass. 'Just one thing: as my father lay dying he bequeathed me some writing, and I have it here, etched upon the shoe on my hind hoof. Come, sir wolf, read it out for me and tell me what it says, and after that you can eat me all you please.'

He raised his hind leg and, as the wolf peered to read, kicked him a hefty thwack on the snout, and the wolf found himself at sea and floundering. The fox, seeing this, took fright and leapt into the briny sea of her own accord to avoid the ass's kick, and so she and the wolf both drowned, while the boat was left adrift, out at sea, with just its cargo of olives, and the ass...

Sources

Traditional storytelling was first recorded in Greek-speaking lands by pioneering ethnographers Nicolaos Politis (1852–1921) and Georgios Megas (1893–1976). Numerous collections of Greek folk tales have been published since, and new editions continue to appear. Here is a representative sample:

Nikolaos G. Politis, *Παραδόσεις: Μελέται περί του βίου και της γλώσσης του ελληνικού λαού, τ. Α'* [Traditions: Studies regarding the life and the language of the Greek people, vol. i]. Athens: Historical Research Publications, 1904.

Georgios A. Megas, *Ελληνικά Παραμύθια* [Greek Fairy Tales]. Athens: Hestia Publishers, 1927.

Georgios A. Megas, *Ελληνικά Παραμύθια, Σειρά Δευτέρα* [Greek Fairy Tales, vol. ii]. Athens: Hestia Publishers, 1962.

Anna Angelopoulou, *Ελληνικά παραμύθια Α'* [Greek Fairy Tales, vol. i]. Athens: Hestia Publishers, 1991.

Anna Angelopoulou, *Ελληνικά παραμύθια Β'* [Greek Fairy Tales, vol. ii]. Athens: Hestia Publishers, 2004.

Kostas Kafantaris, *Ελληνικά Παραμύθια, Βιβλίο πρώτο,* [Greek Fairy Tales, vol. i]. Athens: Potamos, 2005.

Kostas Kafantaris, *Ελληνικά Παραμύθια, Βιβλίο δεύτερο,* [Greek Fairy Tales, vol. ii]. Athens: Potamos, 2005.

MODERN
GREEK
CLASSICS

aiorabooks.com

C.P. CAVAFY

Selected Poems

BILINGUAL EDITION

Translated by David Connolly

Cavafy is by far the most translated and well-known Greek poet internationally. Whether his subject matter is historical, philosophical or sensual, Cavafy's unique poetic voice is always recognizable by its ironical, suave, witty and world-weary tones.

STRATIS DOUKAS

A Prisoner of War's Story

Translated by Petro Alexiou
With an Afterword by Dimitris Tziovas

Smyrna, 1922: A young Anatolian Greek is taken prisoner at the end of the Greek–Turkish War. A classic tale of survival in a time of nationalist conflict, *A Prisoner of War's Story* is a beautifully crafted and pithy narrative. Affirming the common humanity of peoples, it earns its place among Europe's finest anti-war literature of the post-WWI period.

ODYSSEUS ELYTIS

1979 NOBEL PRIZE FOR LITERATURE

In the Name of Luminosity and Transparency

With an Introduction by Dimitris Daskalopoulos

The poetry of Odysseus Elytis owes as much to the ancients and Byzantium as to the surrealists of the 1930s, bringing romantic modernism and structural experimentation to Greece. Collected here are the two speeches Elytis gave on his acceptance of the 1979 Nobel Prize for Literature.

NIKOS ENGONOPOULOS

Cafés and Comets After Midnight and Other Poems

BILINGUAL EDITION

Translated by David Connolly

Derided for his innovative and, at the time, often incomprehensible modernist experiments, Engonopoulos is today regarded as one of the most original artists of his generation. In both his painting and poetry, he created a peculiarly Greek surrealism, a blending of the Dionysian and Apollonian.

M. KARAGATSIS

The Great Chimera

Translated by Patricia Barbeito

A psychological portrait of a young French woman, Marina, who marries a sailor and moves to the island of Syros. Her fate grows entwined with that of the boats and when economic downturn arrives, it brings passion, life and death in its wake.

KOSTAS KARYOTAKIS

Ballad for the Unsung Poets of the Ages

BILINGUAL EDITION

Translated by Simon Darragh

Karyotakis is the poet most emblematic of the turbulent interwar period in Greece. His poetry is often pessimistic and bitingly satirical. His writing combines reverie with sarcasm, a stifling sense of everyday reality with poignant irony. This is verse that is both piercing and resonant.

STELIOS KOULOGLOU

Never Go to the Post Office Alone

Translated by Joshua Barley

A foreign correspondent in Moscow queues at the city's central post office one morning in 1989, waiting to send a fax to his newspaper in New York. With the Soviet Union collapsing and the Berlin Wall about to fall, this moment of history would change the world, and his life, forever.

ANDREAS LASKARATOS

Reflections

BILINGUAL EDITION

Translated by Simon Darragh

Andreas Laskaratos was a writer and poet, a social thinker and, in many ways, a controversialist. His *Reflections* sets out, in a series of calm, clear and pithy aphorisms, his uncompromising and finely reasoned beliefs on morality, justice, personal conduct, power, tradition, religion and government.

MARGARITA LIBERAKI

The Other Alexander

Translated by Willis Barnstone and Elli Tzalopoulou Barnstone

A tyrannical father leads a double life; he has two families and gives the same first names to both sets of children. The half-siblings meet, love, hate, and betray one another. Hailed by Albert Camus as "true poetry," Liberaki's sharp, riveting prose consolidates her place in European literature.

ALEXANDROS PAPADIAMANDIS

Fey Folk

Translated by David Connolly

Alexandros Papadiamandis holds a special place in the history of Modern Greek letters, but also in the heart of the ordinary reader. *Fey Folk* follows the humble lives of quaint, simple-hearted folk living in accordance with centuries-old traditions, described here with both reverence and humour.

ALEXANDROS RANGAVIS

The Notary

Translated by Simon Darragh

A mystery set on the island of Cephalonia, this classic work of Rangavis is an iconic tale of suspense and intrigue, love and murder. *The Notary* is Modern Greek literature's contribution to the tradition of early crime fiction, alongside E.T.A. Hoffman, Edgar Allan Poe and Wilkie Collins.

EMMANUEL ROÏDES
Pope Joan
Translated by David Connolly

This satirical novel, a masterpiece of modern Greek literature, retells the legend of a female pope as a disguised criticism of the Orthodox Church of the nineteenth century. It was a bestseller across Europe at its time and the controversy it provoked led to the swift excommunication of its author.

ANTONIS SAMARAKIS
The Flaw
Translated by Simon Darragh

A man is seized from his afternoon drink at the Cafe Sport by two agents of the Regime by car toward Special Branch Headquarters, and the interrogation that undoubtedly awaits him there. Part thriller and part political satire, *The Flaw* has been translated into more than thirty languages.

GEORGE SEFERIS
1979 NOBEL PRIZE FOR LITERATURE
Novel and Other Poems
BILINGUAL EDITION
Translated by Roderick Beaton

Often compared during his lifetime to T.S. Eliot, Seferis is noted for his spare, laconic, dense and allusive verse. Seferis better than any other writer expresses the dilemma experienced by his countrymen then and now: how to be at once Greek and modern.

MAKIS TSITAS
God is My Witness
Translated by Joshua Barley

A hilariously funny and achingly sad portrait of Greek society during the crisis years, as told by a lovable anti-hero. Fifty-year-old Chrysovalantis, who has recently lost his job and struggles with declining health, sets out to tell the story of his life, roaming the streets of Athens on Christmas Eve.

ILIAS VENEZIS

Serenity

Translated by Joshua Barley

The novel follows the journey of a group of Greek refugees from Asia Minor who settle in a village near Athens. It details the hatred of war, the love of nature that surrounds them, the hostility of their new neighbours and eventually their adaptation to a new life.

GEORGIOS VIZYENOS

Thracian Tales

Translated by Peter Mackridge

These short stories bring to life Vizyenos' native Thrace. Through masterful psychological portayals, each story keeps the reader in suspense to the very end: Where did Yorgis' grandfather travel on his only journey? What was Yorgis' mother's sin? Who was responsible for his brother's murder?

GEORGIOS VIZYENOS

Moskov Selim

Translated by Peter Mackridge

A novella by Georgios Vizyenos, one of Greece's best-loved writers, set in Thrace during the time of the Russo-Turkish War, whose outcome would decide the future of southeastern Europe. *Moskov Selim* is a moving tale of kinship, despite the gulf of nationality and religion.

NIKIFOROS VRETTAKOS

Selected Poems

BILINGUAL EDITION

Translated by David Connolly

The poems of Vrettakos are rooted in the Greek landscape and coloured by the Greek light, yet their themes and sentiment are ecumenical. His poetry offers a vision of the paradise that the world could be, but it is also imbued with an awareness of the abyss that the world threatens to become.

AN ANTHOLOGY

Greek Folk Songs BILINGUAL EDITION

Translated by Joshua Barley

The Greek folk songs were passed down from generation to generation in a centuries-long oral tradition, lasting until the present. Written down at the start of the nineteenth century, they became the first works of modern Greek poetry, playing an important role in forming the country's modern language and literature.

AN ANTHOLOGY

Rebetika: Songs from the Old Greek Underworld BILINGUAL EDITION

Translated by Katharine Butterworth & Sara Schneider

The songs in this book are a sampling of the urban folk songs of Greece during the first half of the twentieth century. Often compared to American blues, rebetika songs are the creative expression of people living a marginal and often underworld existence on the fringes of established society.